Explanation and Interaction

ACL–MIT Press Series in Natural Language Processing
Aravind K. Joshi, Karen Sparck Jones, and Mark Y. Liberman, editors

Speaking: From Intention to Articulation, by Willem J. M. Levelt

Plan Recognition in Natural Language Dialogue, by Sandra Carberry

Cognitive Models of Speech Processing: Psycholinguistic and Computational Perspectives, edited by Gerry T. M. Altmann

Computational Morphology: Practical Mechanisms for the English Lexicon, by Graeme D. Ritchie, Graham J. Russell, Alan W. Black, and Stephen G. Pulman

The Core Language Engine, edited by Hiyan Alshawi

Morphology and Computation, by Richard Sproat

Generating Referring Expressions: Constructing Descriptions in a Domain of Objects and Processes, by Robert Dale

The Logical Approach to Syntax: Foundations, Specifications, and Implementations of Theories of Government and Binding, by Edward P. Stabler, Jr.

Explanation and Interaction: The Computer Generation of Explanatory Dialogues, by Alison Cawsey

Explanation and Interaction
The Computer Generation of Explanatory Dialogues

Alison Cawsey

A Bradford Book
The MIT Press
Cambridge, Massachusetts
London, England

This book was printed and bound in the United States of America.

Library of Congress Cataloging-in-Publication Data
Cawsey, Alison.
  Explanation and interaction : the computer generation of explanatory dialogues / Alison Cawsey.
      p.   cm.
  Includes bibliographical references and index.
  ISBN 0-262-03202-3
  1. Human-computer interaction. 2. Question-answering systems. 3. Natural language processing (Computer science) I. Title.
QA76.9.H85C38   1993
006.3'3—dc20   92-35405
                                                                          CIP

Contents

Acknowledgments

This book is based on research carried out at the Department of Artificial Intelligence, University of Edinburgh, for my doctoral thesis. I would like to thank my supervisors, Peter Ross and Paul Brna, and all my other colleagues at Edinburgh, for the many different ways they have contributed to the research and the environment there. In particular, Chris Mellish provided helpful comments and encouragement as I completed my thesis and developed it as a book. The research was supported by a Studentship and Fellowship from the Science and Engineering Research Council.

The final preparation of this book was carried out while working at the University of Cambridge Computer Laboratory, and I especially thank my colleagues there for allowing me time to finish it. Karen Sparck Jones, in particular, provided helpful advice and encouragement.

Finally, I would like to thank Richard, for being Richard.

1 Introduction

Explanations are important in many areas of human-computer interaction. For example, advisory systems may need to explain why a particular course of action is appropriate, and expert systems may need to explain their line of reasoning in order to justify some conclusion. The purpose of tutoring and help systems may be to explain some material, such as how to do a complex task, or how something works.

Whatever type of explanation is being given, there is a danger that it will not be understood. It is therefore important that users be able to ask for clarification. In a long and complex explanation they should be able to interrupt part way through and sort out any problems before the explanation proceeds, while the explainer should keep a check on the user's apparent understanding, and adjust the level of the explanation as appropriate.

In this book we present a computational model of explanation generation which takes account of its essentially interactive nature. The model has been used in a system to generate extended interactive explanations of circuit behavior, but could be applied to the computer generation of interactive explanations in a wide range of application areas.

1.1 The Problem

In order to make clear what problem this book addresses, we should show both what we mean by explanation and what problems are involved in generating interactive explanations.

In general an explanation is something which makes some piece of knowledge clear to the hearer. For example, answers to the following are all types of explanations (adapted from [Dra88]):

- Explain how to get to Edinburgh.
- Explain how to mend a puncture.
- Explain why you were late home last night.
- Explain how a television works.

In each of these cases there is a coherent piece of knowledge to convey. The explanation is complete when the hearer is satisfied with the reply and understands the piece of knowledge. In some cases a brief phrase may be all that is needed, but in others the explanation may be very complex, taking many minutes.

Verbal explanations of all lengths are intrinsically interactive. The explainer will frequently not know enough about the hearer's background knowledge or their explanatory need to be able to give a satisfactory explanation in one go. The hearer will often have to ask further questions until they understand what they have been told and have all the information that they require. For short explanations this results in an *explanatory dialogue* consisting of an initial, potentially complete explanation and a sequence of follow-up questions and responses. An example explanatory dialogue of this type, taken from transcripts of human verbal explanations of circuit behavior, is given below:[1]

E: 1. In this circuit we have an output whose voltage depends on the amount of light falling on the LDR, and the more light falls on here the more it will conduct, so the higher the voltage will be here.

N: 2. What does LDR stand for?

E: 3. Light dependent resistor.

N: 4. What's this bit?

E: 5. That bit's a variable resistor so you can change how the output level varies with the resistance of the LDR.

N: 6. Say that again.

E: 7. Well, this is a potential divider here, so the potential here will be between zero and 9V in proportion to the resistance of these two things.

N: 8. What's potential?

E: 9. The voltage.

This type of explanatory dialogue has been discussed by Moore [Moo89, Moo91], who presents an approach to explanation generation where follow-up questions can be dealt with in the context of the previous explanation. Her system is concerned primarily with expert system explanations, where a short explanation may be required to justify the system's conclusions or recommendations.

When a longer explanation is required it becomes important to check the hearer's understanding as the explanation progresses, and to allow the hearer to interrupt with clarification questions.[2] These interactions

---

[1] In this and later examples "E" refers to the expert (or explainer), and "N" refers to the novice (or explainee). We will indicate sentences which have been interrupted in some way by ".." and omitted sections by "[...]".

[2] We will use the term "hearer" to refer to the recipient of a human verbal explanation, whether or not they are passively listening.

allow the explainer to update assumptions about the hearer's knowledge, and to continue the explanation in a more appropriate manner.
For example, it would be quite possible to discover, a few utterances
into explaining how a television worked, that the hearer had no physics
background. The explainer would take this into account and continue
the explanation in a non-technical manner.

In this book we are concerned with how these latter kinds of extended
explanatory dialogues may be generated. This includes considering how
interactions with the user may be managed within them, how assumptions about the user's knowledge may be updated on the basis of these
interactions, and how these changing assumptions may influence the
continuing explanation.

To get an idea of some of the problems involved, consider the dialogue
fragment below, again taken from the transcripts (but illustrating a more
extended explanation):

E: 1. These components here, you might consider them as being both resistors. Two variable resistors. I can write down a relation for resistance..

N: 2. You'll have to tell me what a resistor is.

E: 3. A resistor is an element which if you apply a voltage across it there is
a certain current flowing through the resistor. There is a relationship
$V = I \times R$..

N: 4. It doesn't help. What does it do? Does it stop the current getting
through?

E: 5. Yes. If the resistance was nil it would just be a connection here, then
the current is mainly restricted by the amount of current.. voltage..

N: 6. Right, so the resistor has to be, can be of various strengths presumably.
And the current going through it has to be of certain strengths before
it can get through the resistor?

E: 7. No, in this case the current is determined by the strength of your power
supply and you can rewrite this relation to $I = V \div R$, where if this
is constant, say 10V or 9V battery for example, changing this resistor
changes the current through the resistor. If this one becomes nil you
get an infinite current. If it's high then the current becomes low.

N: 8. I see, or at least I think I see.

E: 9. Well, this circuit here are just two resistors, switched in serial mode.
You can think of it as one resistor supplied with a voltage 9V, and there
will be a current flowing through the circuit.

In this example the expert (E) was in the middle of explaining to the
novice (N) how a simple circuit involving two variable resistors worked.

However, in this case the expert had misjudged the novice's level of expertise in this topic, assuming her to be familiar with basic circuit components such as resistors. Fortunately the novice has the opportunity to interrupt and seek clarification when the unfamiliar concept is introduced. After a fairly complex clarification sequence the novice eventually (in utterance 8) indicates that she understands, and the expert resumes the explanation of the circuit's behavior.

This example introduces a number of problems for the computer generation of interactive explanations, including:

• How can the system best tailor an explanation to the user's assumed level of expertise? For example, how should the above explanation of circuit behavior differ for the complete novice and for the relative expert in the domain?

• How and when should the user be able to interrupt a complex explanation? Should they be given the chance after every utterance, or just at the end of an explanation?

• How can the system keep a check on the user's understanding of the explanation, and update assumptions about their level of expertise? In the dialogue above, for example, the expert should perhaps revise the assumption that they are familiar with the basic concepts of electricity after utterance 2, while after utterance 8 the expert might assume that they now probably understand what resistors are.

• How should the system continue an explanation after an interruption? The system may not have completed the main explanation, but the user may have introduced new topics, and old assumptions about their level of expertise may no longer apply. How can it continue a coherent explanation given this changing context?

It is issues like these that we set out to address in this book. While there has been a significant amount of work recently on generating coherent multi-sentence descriptions based on an analysis of written texts (e.g., [McK85, Par88, Hov88]), there has been very little on generating interactive discourse based on human verbal explanations or descriptions. As we can see from the example above, this presents new problems and requires new solutions.

1.2   The Approach

The overall goal of this work is to present an approach for the computer generation of interactive explanations which addresses issues such as those discussed above. This involves deciding what to say in an explanation, deciding how to manage the dialogue, and deciding how to update any assumptions about the user. This section will outline the approach taken to this problem.

Interactive explanations may be viewed as a kind of goal-oriented dialogue, where the goal of the explainer is to make clear to the hearer some complex piece of knowledge. The problem is therefore that of determining how this overall goal may result in a particular sequence of dialogue actions, depending on aspects of the discourse situation such as the user's assumed knowledge. Determining how an overall goal may result in a sequence of actions is essentially a planning problem, and both the content of the explanation and the organization of the dialogue will be determined by a set of planning rules. Most traditional AI planning systems construct an entire course of action to achieve some target change in the state of the world. This plan may then be separately executed. However, in an uncertain and changing environment the execution of such a plan may not succeed, as the state of the world may have changed unexpectedly since the plan was constructed. There are various possible approaches for dealing with this problem. First, a conditional plan may be created, with alternative branches appropriate for different situations. If none of the conditions hold then the planner may be reinvoked, to patch the plan. Second, a system can interleave planning and execution in some way, so that observed changes in, or better information about, the state of the world will influence further planning. Third, a system may be provided with reactive strategies for dealing with particular situations as they occur. These different approaches are reviewed in [Geo90] for example.

In an explanatory dialogue assumptions about the "state of the world" (i.e., the user's knowledge) are highly uncertain, being refined and revised in the context of an interaction. For example, if the user asks a question in the middle of an explanation then this may cause the system's assessment of their knowledge to change. A conditional plan would have to be highly complex to deal with all the possible interactions and consequent changes in the user model. We therefore take the approach of

interleaving planning and execution, with further strategies for reacting
to problems and misunderstandings as they arise.

The type of planning involved is very simple. (In fact, those within
the AI planning community might be reluctant to call it "planning.")
An explanation plan is developed top down and depth first, from the
top level explanation goal down to simple graphical or textual actions,
using planning rules to expand goals into subgoals. As soon as primitive
actions are planned they are immediately realized, while an agenda of
partially ordered explanation goals is used to represent the remaining
explanation yet to be generated.

Two sets of planning rules are used. Content planning rules determine the overall content of the dialogue, while dialogue planning rules
determine the domain independent structure of the dialogue.such as the
organization of different types of exchanges with the user.

The planning process may be influenced by the discourse context. It
will influence which goal is taken off the agenda, which planning rule
is selected, and which subgoals it attempts to satisfy. The discourse
context includes the assumptions about the user's knowledge, the current
objects in *focus*, and the roles of the participants. Depending on the
user's assumed current knowledge, different explanation strategies will
be selected, prerequisite information either included or left out, and
different exchanges with the user selected. The order of the explanation
will be influenced by the current discourse focus, while aspects of the
dialogue organization will be influenced by the roles of the participants
(e.g., tutor-tutee, advisor-advisee).

Interactions with the user may result in new goals being put on the
agenda and subdialogues planned to achieve those goals. These interactions may in turn cause a change both in assumptions about the
user's knowledge and in the current discourse focus. As the planning
proceeds incrementally, with planning and execution interleaved, interactions with the user will also influence the details of the future explanation plan. This will include changing the default order, selecting
explanation strategies different from those which would otherwise have
been selected, including different prerequisite information, and selecting
different exchanges with the user.

The type of simple planning process used — essentially the decomposition of goals into subgoals by selecting from alternative specialized
planning rules — has sometimes been referred to as skeletal planning (cf.

[FI85]). It is not as powerful as traditional AI planning techniques, but is efficient (running in approximately linear time, where doubling the length of an explanation will double the amount of processing involved) and appears consistent with the approach taken by human experts for expert or routine performance at tasks [CMN83, SY88]. Limitations of the approach will be discussed in chapter 7.

The simple incremental planning approach taken may be viewed as a compromise between planning things out fully before beginning an utterance (as with most existing systems which generate multi-sentence texts), and simply reacting to situations as they occur in a dialogue, with no clear idea of the future discourse (as with most existing dialogue systems). Although there are problems and limitations it appears to be a promising basic approach for generating flexible tailored interactive explanations.

The basic architecture of the discourse generator developed[3] is illustrated in figure 1.1. In the diagram we see that the user model (in this case, simply the set of assumptions about the user's knowledge) and the discourse model (representing the past and partially planned future discourse) are both updated by and influence the planning of the discourse. The discourse planner also uses the dialogue and content planning rules and a representation of the relevant domain knowledge. (In the implemented system there are about 50 planning rules and 14 domain objects.) The agenda of explanation goals yet to be fulfilled is used as the main controlling data structure, being continually revised as planning proceeds.

The main input to the system is an explanation goal (such as to explain how a particular circuit works), while interactions with the user provide additional inputs and cause additional goals to be set. The output of the system is a sequence of dialogue actions which may result in both text and graphics being displayed.

We should make it clear at this point that this book does not address issues concerning the generation or interpretation of natural language sentences. In the implemented system described, we use a menu-based interface for user input, and a simple template-based approach for system output. The natural language sentences in example system dia-

---

[3]Referred to from now on as EDGE (Explanatory Discourse GEnerator).

logues (such as that given in the next section) are therefore based on these menu selections and filled templates.

1.3   Example System Dialogue

The EDGE discourse planner has been fully implemented and used to generate interactive explanations of circuit behavior. To illustrate how the different components in the system are used, we shall go through a short example dialogue generated by the system:[4]

S: 1. Right, I'm going to explain how the light detector unit works.
   2. Do you know what it is like?
U: 3. No.
S: 4. Well, It is a kind of potential divider circuit.
   5. It has the following components:
   6. – A fixed resistor.
   7. – A light-dependent resistor.
U: 8. What's this component here?
S: 9. Well, This component here is a light-dependent resistor.
  10. When it has a high input light intensity its output resistance is quite low.
  11. When it has a low input light intensity its output resistance is quite high.
  12. This component here is a fixed resistor.
  13. The light detector unit's function is to produce an output voltage that depends on its input light intensity.
  14. Now, Suppose its input light intensity is high.
    [...]
  22. Enough about how the light detector unit works?
U: 23. OK.

In this example the system was initially set the goal of explaining to the user how a particular circuit (a light detector unit) worked. The system therefore began to plan a dialogue to achieve this goal, using a mixture of dialogue and content planning rules to decide what to say and how to manage the dialogue. First, a high level dialogue planning

---

[4]In this and later example dialogues "S" refers to the system, while "U" refers to the user. The system pauses after each numbered utterance, waiting for the user to interrupt or to indicate that it should continue.

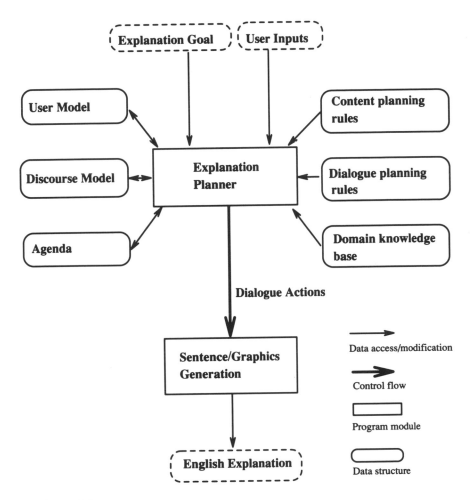

Figure 1.1
Components of the Explanatory Discourse Generator

rule is selected to determine the overall structure of the dialogue. This consists of an opening "exchange" (utterance 1), the main body of the dialogue (utterances 2–21), and a closing exchange (utterances 22–23). In this case the opening exchange is just a statement concerning what the system is about to explain to the user (utterance 1) and the closing exchange (utterances 22–23) is used primarily to check that the user is happy with the explanation and give them a chance to ask follow-up questions.

Once the overall organization of the dialogue has been decided, control passes to the content planning rules to plan the main body of the dialogue. These are used to decide what to include in the explanation and what explanation strategies to use. Choices in content planning depend primarily on the system's assumptions about the user's knowledge, so where this is uncertain the system may question the user as in utterance 2. The main explanation then really begins in utterance 4. Background information about the circuit is given which will help the user understand how it works (utterancs 4–7). Then in utterance 8 the user interrupts with a clarification question.

There are a number of things to note about the clarification sequence. First, both the asking of the question (utterance 8) and the response (utterance 9) involve reference to a diagram to identify the unknown circuit symbol. Such use of graphics and pointing is vital in explanations of device behavior, and will be discussed in chapter 6. Second, the system is able to continue the explanation in a coherent manner after the interruption. If possible the system will attempt to maintain the focus introduced by the user as it continues its explanation after the clarification (utterances 10–11 etc.). Third, the actual content of the continuing explanation may be influenced by the interruption. Any material which has already been covered in the interruption (such as the identification of the light-dependent resistor) is now pruned from the explanation, while if the user's assumed level of expertise has been changed because of the interruption, both the explanation strategies and the detailed content of the continuing explanation may change.

This example illustrates how a simple interactive explanation may be generated, and how the interactions within the explanation may influence the details of the future developing explanation. The principles used in generating this explanation apply to extended explanations of many types, such as task descriptions or advice. Revising the system to generate example dialogues in other domains involves modifying the content planning rules and writing a new knowledge base, but does not require any other changes to the system illustrated in figure 1.1.

1.4 Brief Overview of Related Research

There is a huge amount of research relevant to the task of generating interactive explanations. This includes work on text planning, the organization of dialogue, and user modeling. Some of this background research will be described in more detail in chapters 2–5.

Text planning is concerned with how a coherent, appropriate, multi-sentence text may be generated given some communicative goal. The communicative goal may be of various kinds, such as:

- to **describe** an object.
- to **convince** the hearer to take some action.
- to make the hearer **believe** or **understand** something.

There are often standard strategies for satisfying different kinds of goals. For example, to describe an object it is common to mention the constituents of the object, give characteristic information about each constituent in turn, and then provide additional characteristic information about the object [McK85]. To convince someone to take some action a common strategy is to *recommend* the action, *motivate* it (showing that it is a good thing), and *enable* it (explaining how to do it) [Moo89]. To make sure something is understood it is important to give *background* information first. Research on text planning has been mainly concerned with capturing these strategies, either in terms of *schemata*, capturing the overall organizational patterns of particular types of text [McK85, Par88], or in terms of more general purpose *rhetorical relations* applying between adjacent text spans [Moo89, MP89, Hov88].

Knowledge of dialogue structure is also important for generating interactive explanations. Researchers in different fields have looked at dialogue organization in very different ways. In AI, dialogue is commonly viewed as an aspect of rational, planned action, with the organization of the dialogue resulting fairly directly from the participants' goals (e.g., [Pow79, GS86]). In discourse analysis, the general patterns or structures of particular types of dialogue have been analyzed, and captured in some kind of discourse grammar. In conversation analysis, it is the local organization of conversations that is of primary interest, and how people use the conventions of conversation as a resource, to make sense of language in context and to recover from problems in understanding [Suc87, Lev83, ch. 6]. Each perspective helps us in making sense of and generating interactive explanations.

Finally, work on user modeling is important if we are to generate appropriately tailored explanations and update assumptions about the user's knowledge. Several authors have shown how such assumptions may be updated in the context of a natural language dialogue [KF87, Chi89, WK89]. A common approach (used in the EDGE system) is to start with some *stereotype* based model, where the user's knowledge can be guessed from their general class or level of expertise. This model can then be updated and refined based on particular interactions with the user.

1.5   Guide to Remaining Chapters

The remaining chapters discuss in more detail the background to this work, and show how dialogues such as the one above are generated in the EDGE system.

The approach taken in this work was based in the first instance on an analysis of human explanatory dialogues. This analysis considered both the organization of the content of explanations in a particular domain, and general features of the expert-novice interaction. It was motivated by the belief that it may be possible to provide better computer explanations if we follow some of the conventions and strategies observed in human discourse. The analysis of such explanations is described in chapter 2.

In chapters 3–5 the main issues involved in generating interactive explanations are discussed, and the components of the EDGE interactive explanation system presented. Chapter 3 focuses on how to decide on the content of the explanation, depending on assumptions about the user's knowledge. The components of the EDGE system which are relevant to this are the content planning rules and the planner in figure 1.1. In chapter 4 we go on to discuss the problems of managing interactions with the user as the explanation progresses. Here we focus on the dialogue planning rules in figure 1.1. Chapter 5 extends the approach to consider how assumptions about the user's knowledge can be updated in an explanation, presenting the EDGE user modeling rules.

In chapter 6 we show in more detail how the EDGE system can be applied in the particular domain of explaining how things work. The underlying domain model is described, along with the use of graphical (e.g., pointing) actions. Detailed examples are given of the complete system's operation. Some readers may prefer to start with this chapter, to get a feel for the operation of the whole system.

In chapter 7 the system is evaluated and its contributions assessed. The evaluation consists of both an empirical evaluation, exposing problems with the implemented system, and an assessment of the theoretical limitations of the approach. Some directions for further work are suggested. The discussion of the contributions of the work focuses on a number of possible practical applications.

2 Analyzing Human Explanatory Dialogues

The computational model of explanation generation presented in this book takes as starting point an analysis of human verbal explanations. There are two main reasons why we might develop a computational model based on such an analysis. First, we might be interested in the mechanisms by which humans generate the given explanatory dialogues. We could develop a computational model that explained aspects of that process. Second, we might believe that computer explanation systems might be improved by closer adherence to principles of human discourse. Our computational model might emulate some of the features of human discourse, but need not use the same underlying mechanisms. It is this second reason that we are primarily interested in here — we hope that by developing a model of explanation generation which captures features of human explanations we may eventually be able to provide more flexible and helpful systems for a range of computer applications.

There are many aspects of human explanations which we could analyze. These include aspects of the high level organization of the explanation, and aspects of the way individual propositions are conveyed. In this book we are mainly concerned with the high level organization, including both the organization of the content of the explanation and the organization of the interactions between explainer and hearer.

When analyzing explanation content we were primarily influenced by analyses used as the basis of previous text planning systems. (The systems developed on the basis of these analyses are referred to in chapter 3.) The analysis given in this chapter will be contrasted with this related work. When analyzing dialogue structure we were influenced by previous work on discourse analysis, and to a lesser extent, work on tutorial dialogues. The relevant background work will be briefly described, and we will show how the dialogue phenomena described in these types of analysis can be observed in our corpus of explanatory dialogues.

A corpus of verbal explanations of how simple electronic circuits work is used for these analyses. Our corpus was obtained by asking different experts to each explain the behavior of a set of up to eight electronic circuits. Each expert was supplied with circuit diagrams and a pencil. Seven experts explained to a novice who could contribute to the dialogue in any way desired. This gave a set of 52 interactive explanatory dialogues. Four experts simply explained to the non-participating experimenter, giving a total of 32 non-interactive explanations. These non-interactive explanations allowed the organization of the content to be analyzed more straightforwardly. Each explanation was transcribed, recording the basic "text" of the interaction, but not gestures or intonation. The circuit explanations averaged one (typed) page long each when transcribed.

The explanations obtained are of a fairly restricted type. In general the utterances in an explanatory dialogue will depend on (at least) the subject matter, the roles of the participants (e.g., tutorial), the mode of the interaction (e.g., verbal with visual contact vs. text-based), and the particular goals, knowledge, and interests of the participants (see chapter 3). The explanations in our corpus have the following features:

Subject Matter: How a range of circuits work.

Participant Roles: These varied slightly, as not specified by the experimenter, with some explainers adopting a more explicitly tutorial role than others.

Participant Goals: To make the explainee understand how the circuits worked.

Participant Knowledge and Interests: The knowledge of the participants varied widely across the experiment, but their interests and attitudes, though varied, had minimal apparent impact because of the experimental setting.

Mode of Interaction: The mode of interaction was verbal with visual contact, with both participants able to use pencil and paper and refer to the circuit diagrams provided.

From this corpus of explanations one can make some generalizations concerning explanations in this domain (how circuits work). It seems likely too that these results will partially generalize to explanations of how other sorts of things work. However, many features which we would like to analyze only occur in a small number of the explanations. For example, features of tutorial dialogues only occurred where the participants adopted an explicitly tutorial role. General statements cannot be made about these features — they can only be used as examples of phenomena which exist, and which an explanation system (adopting a tutorial role) should be able to deal with. The corpus is also not large enough to make interesting comparisons concerning how different factors (such as the knowledge of the explainee) affect the explanation, though guesses can be made.

The following two sections describe the analysis of the content of the explanations in the given corpus, and the analysis of features of the dialogue.

2.1 Analyzing Content Organization

This section will discuss how the high level structure of uninterrupted text may be analyzed, focusing on the analysis of the explanations in the corpus described above. The approach to text analysis considered here is based on classifying the clauses in a text in some way, and (given this classification) describing common structures of a range of texts using some kind of discourse grammar (analogous to a grammar of sentence structure).[1] Of course, in general discourse structure is much more weakly constrained than sentence structure, and the "grammar" will only capture the *normal* patterns of discourse in a particular discourse situation. It should not be viewed as any kind of standard that a discourse should fall within in order to be correct.

A single example explanation will be used in much of the discussion and is given in figure 2.1. This example was a verbal explanation given by a physics teacher to the author.

2.1.1 Classifying Utterances

The first step in analyzing the explanations is to classify the different utterances in the explanation. Different types of analysis result in part from the different ways we can classify utterances. For example, if we concentrate on the type of content conveyed in an utterance we could classify statement 1 in figure 2.2 as *identifying* a device as an instance of a particular type. If we concentrate on the *role* played by that utterance in the overall explanation it might be classified as giving some *background* information. Of course, the role played by an utterance is hard to objectively determine, and depends heavily on the utterance context. Many discourse analysts therefore get multiple analysts to classify the utterances in the same text or discourse. A reliable objective analysis is then suggested if each analyst arrives at the same classification.

To be a useful basis for explanation generation the classification of

---

[1] Note that the analysis of dialogue structure may be similarly based on classifying utterances and inferring discourse grammars. Many of the comments below therefore also apply to the analysis of dialogues.

1. Well, this here looks to be a potential divider circuit
2. and it contains two components
3. one of which is a light-dependent resistor
4. and the other is a variable resistor.
5. The function of this circuit is to provide a varying output voltage on this line here.
6. The idea is that when light falls on the light-dependent resistor its resistance changes.
7. So therefore because the resistance of this series circuit has changed, the voltage at this point here can change.
8. So when light falls on the LDR the resistance of this part of the circuit is very low.
9. And so this voltage here is a high voltage.
10. In darkness the resistance of the LDR is large
11. and so the voltage at this point here drops to a low value.
12. So we can get a high or low output depending on how much light is falling on the light-dependent resistor.

Figure 2.1
Example Human Uninterrupted Explanation

Identification	Attributive	Constituency
Evidence	Cause-effect	Renaming
Amplification	Analogy	Generalization
Inference	Explanation	Particular illustration

Figure 2.2
A Subset of McKeown's Rhetorical Predicates

utterances must be general enough so that a range of explanations may
be classified using the same categories, yet constrained enough so that
it may be used as a basis for selecting specific utterances in generation. [2]
For example, categories such as *introduce, summarize,* or *elaborate* appear to be insufficiently constraining on their own, while a category
such as *identify-LDR* would only apply to circuits with an LDR (light-
dependent resistor). A classification scheme should arguably also allow
utterances in a discourse to be assigned unambiguously to a single category. Although this is a difficult criterion to meet, problems with obtaining a unique classification are often the direct result of a confused
classification scheme which mixes different types of category.

In early work on text planning, researchers analyzed text structure
by classifying individual utterances using a set of *rhetorical predicates*
[McK85, Par88]. Some of the rhetorical predicates used in [McK85] are
given in figure 2.1. In principle these predicates are meant to refer to an
utterance's role in the text. However, many of the predicates can also
be viewed as referring to the type of content conveyed in an utterance
(e.g., *cause-effect, identification*), largely independent of textual context,
while others, such as *analogy* and *particular illustration*, can be seen as
describing the *way* these concepts may be conveyed to the hearer. Given
this range of types of "rhetorical predicates" it is difficult to uniquely
classify utterances. An utterance may *identify* an object in order to
provide *background* information, for example, or provide *cause-effect* information using an *analogy*. Because of this difficulty, in our analysis
we describe utterances (or sequences of utterances) using three types of
classification:

---

[2]Another possibility is to use a number of different types of categorization, each
providing different types of constraint on the discourse structure.

- Type of *content*, based on the sort of concepts conveyed in an utterance or utterance sequence, independent of the discourse context (e.g., describing an object's *function*).
- Type of *role*, based on the role an utterance is playing in the whole text (e.g., giving *background* information). This category is based on *relations* between text sections.
- Type of *explanation*, based on the way concepts are conveyed (e.g., using *analogies* or *examples*).

Distinguishing between the first two of these sorts of category seems essential in the analysis of any texts. The third is less clearly distinct. However, for explanatory texts it is useful to consider the way concepts are conveyed, independently of the type of concepts themselves or their role in the overall text. We therefore include it as a separate category in our analysis.

Figure 2.3 illustrates the three sets of categories used. Most of these categories apply to sequences of utterances, rather than just to a single utterance. The categories given are those required for the analysis,[3] and are not intended to cover all types of discourse. Figure 2.4 shows part of the analysis of the example explanation in figure 2.1 using these categories.

2.1.2 Describing Structure: Content Grammars and Schemata

Once the utterances in a set of texts or dialogues have been classified, we can try to obtain a grammar or schema which covers the organization of all (or the vast majority) of the texts/dialogues in the corpus. The resulting grammar or schema will obviously be specific to the type of texts analyzed, but may be compared with the results of other analyses to test the generality of the results. The schemata derived by McKeown [McK85] and by Paris [Par88, Par89] will therefore be described below.

McKeown classified a wide range of object descriptions and produced a set of four schemata which captured all the different structures observed in these textual descriptions. There is considerable flexibility within the schemata, as well as some ambiguity in the classifications, so it is unclear how strong a result this is. However, she was able to use

---

[3]The last *content* category, *component*, doesn't refer to a coherent *type* of information, but more to the relationships between the objects in the description. It nonetheless provides a useful high level characterization of the content of a section of an object description.

Type of Role/Rhetorical Relation:

Background	Summary/conclusion	Elaboration
Compare-contrast	Sequence	

Type of Content:

How-it-works	Structure	Process
Behavior	Identification	Constituency
Function	Causal-event	Component(s)

Type of Explanation:

Examples	Classification	Analogy

Figure 2.3
Categories Used in Analyzing Explanations

these schemata effectively to generate coherent multi-sentence texts. An example schema is given in figure 2.5. [4]

Paris focused on how descriptions of physical devices depended on the class of user they were aimed at. She compared descriptions given in sources aimed at novices (e.g., children's encyclopedias and text books) with those given in sources aimed at relative experts (e.g., adult encyclopedias and repair manuals), abstracting schemata capturing the structure of the texts in each [Par88]. These are illustrated in figure 2.6. The schema derived from the children's encyclopedias is based on a description of the *processes* involved as the device functions, while that derived from the adults' encyclopedias is based more on the object's *structure*, more or less following McKeown's *constituency* schema. Based on these results she suggests that device descriptions aimed at novices should be based on the process schema, and those aimed at experts should be based on the revised *constituency* schema. She argues that this is because experts can *infer* process from structure, given general knowledge of the domain.

McKeown's and Paris's schemata arguably mix types of category, as mentioned above. Most of the categories relate to the type of information being conveyed, yet others refer more to the *role* of the utterance

---

[4]Note that "/" indicates optional alternatives, "+" indicates that the item may appear 1 to n times, "*" indicates 0 to n times and "{}" optionality.

Utterance	Content Type
1. Well, this here looks to be a potential divider circuit	identification (1–5 = structure)
2. and it contains two components,	constituency
3. one of which is a light-dependent resistor	
4. and the other is a variable resistor	
5. The function of this circuit is to provide a varying output voltage on this line here.	function
6. The idea is that when light falls on the light-dependent resistor its resistance changes.	causal-event (6–7 = process)
7. So therefore because the resistance of this series circuit has changed, the voltage at this point here can change.	causal-event
8. So when light falls on the LDR the resistance of this part of the circuit is very low.	causal-event (8–9 = process)
9. And so this voltage here is a high voltage.	causal-event
10. In darkness the resistance of the LDR is large	causal-event (10–11 = process)
11. and so the voltage at this point here drops to a low value.	causal-event
12. So we can get a high or low output depending on how much light is falling on the light-dependent resistor.	behavior

Role of Utterances

Utterances 1–5 provide *background* material for the description in utterances 6–11, while utterance 12 provides a *summary* or *conclusion*. There are *sequence* relations between utterances 6 and 7, between 8 and 9 and between 10 and 11.

Explanation Strategies

Explanation strategies involved included *classifying* the circuit as an instance of some class and providing *example* processes to explain how it worked.

Figure 2.4
Analysis of Example Explanation

Constituency
Cause-effect*/Attributive*/
  { Depth-identification/Depth-attributive
    {Particular-illustration/Evidence}
    {Comparison/Analogy}}$^+$
{Amplification/Explanation/Attributive/Analogy}

Figure 2.5
McKeown's Constituency Schema

Revised Constituency Schema

1) *Identify* the item as a member of some generic class.
2) Present the *constituents* of the item to be defined.
3) Present information about each constituent in turn.
4) Present additional information about the item to be defined.

Process Schema

(For each object, given a chain of causal links.)
1) Follow the next causal link.
2) {Mention an important side link.}
3) {Give *attributive* information about a part just introduced.}
4) {Follow substeps if there are any.}
5) Go back to (1).

Figure 2.6
Paris's Constituency and Process Schemata

(e.g., *elaboration*) or to the *way* that a concept may be conveyed (e.g., *analogy*). Mixing category type makes it hard to explain *why* the text has the observed structure, and therefore to generalize the results. In our analysis of the circuit explanations we therefore consider three types of category independently. However, we focus on the type of content (or information) being conveyed. The range of content structures are represented using simple grammar rules (similar to those used by Rumelhart [Rum75] in his story grammars), where each element in a rule is a content type (e.g., causal-event). Grammar rules have the same representational power as schemata, but tend to capture the hierarchical structure of the discourse more clearly, showing how one type of category may be composed of other types.

Figure 2.7 gives the resulting grammar abstracted from our analysis of the non-interactive explanations.[5] The rules capture the order of items in an explanation *if they occur*. However, almost all the items in the rules are optional. For example, in some explanations only the structure was given, in some only the process, and in many both. The figure does not represent the objects involved in the explanation — the *behavior* mentioned in the fifth rule is obviously the behavior of the relevant component, and different from the behavior (of the main device) mentioned in the first rule.

The grammar captures all except one of the uninterrupted explanations, the exception being where the *constituency* was given before *identification*. Most of the interactive explanations also followed the same basic pattern, though the content structure was harder to analyze given extensive user interruptions.

It should be clear how the example explanation in figure 2.1 fits this grammar. The *identification, constituency, function, process(es), behavior* sequence identified in figure 2.4 directly fits the first two rules, while each *process* consists of *causal-events*, as described in the sixth rule. Other, less coherent explanations also fit the same basic pattern. For example, the following text also consists of an *identification, constituency,* and a simple *process* (or *behavior?*) consisting of *causal-events*:

1. Right, potential divider,
2. thermistor temperature dependent, resistor.

---

[5]Note that our category *structure* does not just contain structural information. It is defined to also include component behaviors and device function, for example.

How-it-works → Structure, Process, Behaviour

Structure → Identification, Components, Function

Structure → Similarity, Component-Differences

Components → Constituency, Component$^+$

Component → Identification, Behavior

Process → Causal-event$^+$ (sequence)

Behavior → Causal-event$^+$ (examples)

Figure 2.7
EDGE Explanation Content Grammar

3. So, the output is going to vary between what, I can't think, the.., so the numbers are difficult, but what you're going to have, of the order of, you're going to have between.. Basically the output is going to vary with temperature..

4. So if the resistance on that one drops, that means we're going to get a higher output.

At this point we should contrast the grammar given in figure 2.7 with Paris's schemata. Paris observed structural and process descriptions to be essentially alternatives, depending on the expertise of the reader. The grammar in figure 2.7 suggests instead that both process and structural descriptions commonly occur in an explanation, with the structural description preceding the process description. This difference can be partially explained if we consider further *why* the different types of information are included (discussed further in the next section). A structural description can be viewed as prerequisite information, which a novice should know in order to make sense of a process description, and so may be important in a tutorial explanation. On the other hand, as Paris observed, a true expert could infer the process from the structure. In a non-tutorial context, where the explainer aims only to *describe* the object, including the full structure+process information may be redundant. The content of the explanation depends on the detailed goals of the explainer and on the particular concept they are trying to get across, as well as the assumed knowledge of the hearer. It may include a structure+process description, or just structure, or just process.

The grammar developed ignores the two other types of category of text items that were introduced in the last section — the role of an utterance (or sequence) and the way concepts are conveyed. In our corpus the following was apparent:

- The *structural* description appeared to serve in the role of providing *background* knowledge necessary for the *process* description.
- The final *behavior* description served in the role of giving a *summary* following the *process* description.[6]
- The *structural* description could be presented either using the approach of identifying an objects *class* and then presenting distinguishing attributes (i.e., specific components and function), or by giving an *comparison* with a similar device and giving the contrasting features.

In the first two points above we informally characterize the *role* of text sections. More comprehensive analysis of such functional relations between text sections has been proposed in work on rhetorical relations, and in particular *Rhetorical Structure Theory* (RST) [MT87a]. Mann and Thomson have proposed a set of about 23 rhetorical relations which may occur between text sections, including *background* and *sequence*, and these have been used as the basis of text planning systems [Moo89, Hov88]. However, in our experience such relations on their own provide an insufficiently fine-grained description of text structure not easily adapted to generating particular types of text in a particular domain. Indeed, Mann observes [Man87] that the sorts of descriptions and explanations considered by McKeown [McK85] (similar to those considered here) make relatively little use of such rhetorical relations — most of the relations would have to be encoded as versions of the *elaboration* relation. We therefore base our analysis and text planning primarily on a simple content grammar, with rhetorical relations playing a less prominent role.

---

[6]An alternative analysis which could be considered is to view the *process* description as having an *explanatory* role with respect to the description of behavior. However, as the behavior is normally unknown until the process is explained a summary/conclusion relation appears more appropriate.

2.1.3   Explaining Structure: Plans and Discourse Models

Linking the role played by a text section (e.g., *background* or *summary*) with the type of information conveyed in that text section goes half way toward explaining the discourse structures observed. In particular we can note that the *structure* description provides vital *prerequisite* information for the *process* description, explaining its *background* role. This prerequisite material includes knowledge of the device type, and knowledge of the behavior of the device components.

The grammar rules in figure 2.7 can also be viewed as representing subskill relationships between types of concept. For example, knowing the behavior of a device involves the subskills of knowing what it does (i.e., a *causal-event*) for different *example* input values (seventh rule in the figure).

It appears then that we can explain our discourse grammar in terms of subskill and prerequisite relationships between types of concept being explained. Grammar rules can therefore be rewritten as simple planning rules for making particular types of concept known. Explaining the rules in this way both provides a better basis for generating explanations in other domains without such exhaustive analysis, and allows us to better tailor explanations given knowledge of the user's prior knowledge — if a prerequisite skill is already understood, it need not be included in the explanation.

The planning rules used are discussed in chapters 3 and 6, with a working subset given in appendix B. The range of possible text structures which can be generated should be a subset of those captured by the grammar rules in figure 2.7. Figure 2.8 illustrates a simplified version of the top level planning rule used. The rule corresponds to the first line in the grammar. The prerequisite *structure* is only explained when not already understood. There should be a *summary* relationship between the *process* and *behavior* subgoals, though this is not represented in this simplified example rule.

2.1.4   Conclusion

This section has shown how the organization of the content of simple explanations of circuit behavior may be analyzed and grammar rules developed which capture the observed structure. The observed structure was similar to that discussed by Paris [Par88], and the differences could

```
c-plan how-it-works (device)
   preconditions: know-user structure (device)
   subgoals: c-goal process (device)
            c-goal behavior (device)
```

Figure 2.8
Top Level Planning Rule for Explaining How Things Work

possibly be explained by the different goals of the explainers and assumptions about the hearers' knowledge. The structure of the explanations appeared to be based on subskill and prerequisite relationships between the concepts being explained, and planning rules could be written which captured these relationships. These will provide the basis for the planning of text content described in the next chapter. This approach to explanation planning assumes that there is some high level concept to be explained, and the explainer plans the text by considering both what prerequisite concepts must be explained first, and how to explain the concept in terms of a number of simpler concepts.

The analysis in this section is based on a small corpus and the detailed results may not generalize widely. However, it provides an adequate basis for the development of a text planning system in the particular domain of explaining how things work, and begins to show how text structure relates to the relationship between the concepts in the domain.

2.2   Analyzing Dialogue Structure

So far we have considered the organization of the text content, concentrating on non-interactive explanations. However, this book is concerned with explanations which involve interactions with a novice. This section will therefore be concerned with analyzing features of the explanatory dialogues obtained involving an expert explaining to a novice.

In order to develop a computational model we need to consider both the organization of interactions with the user, and how that organization fits in with the organization of the content. When analyzing the organization of the interactions our starting point will be a theory of tutorial discourse structure, which will be extended and adapted to deal with ex-

planatory dialogues of various types. When considering how this relates
to the content organization we will be considering how far the content
of an explanatory dialogue follows the same structure as the content of
a non-interactive explanation, and how the user's clarification questions
fit into this pattern.

Some of the dialogue features discussed in this section only occurred in
a small number of explanatory dialogues. We therefore aim to develop a
dialogue model that can accommodate these different features, without
requiring them to be present. Numerous examples of these different
dialogue features will be included, and we will discuss how their presence
may depend on the role adopted by the explainer.

2.2.1   Describing the Organization of Interactions

Our starting point when analyzing the organization of the interactions
between explainer and explainee will be a model of tutorial discourse
proposed by Sinclair and Coulthard [SC75]. Although this model is
concerned with more formal discourse, where one teacher is explaining
to a number of students, the basic framework can be usefully applied
to interactive explanations. As in tutorial discourse, in an interactive
explanation there is often one person who dominates the interaction
(the explainer) and the goal of the interaction is to make some body of
knowledge clear to the explainee or student.

Sinclair and Coulthard aimed to develop a grammar capturing possible sequences of interactions given a restricted discourse type. Their
initial work focused on classroom discourse, and a large number of classroom dialogues were analyzed by classifying utterances and sequences of
utterances according to their function in the interaction. For example,
an utterance which *initiated* an exchange with another participant would
be classified as an *initiation* move, while a sequence of utterances closing
some discussion would be classified as a closing *boundary* exchange. The
analysis was somewhat subjective, but it was claimed that a number of
researchers came up with the same classification.

The result of the analysis was a grammar representing the normal
structure of classroom discourse. This grammar describes both the possible sequences of different types of exchanges between the teacher and
students, and the internal structure of these types of exchanges. It is
based on five levels of discourse structure. The first of these is the *lesson*. A lesson consists of a number of *transactions* (such as informing

or directing on some topic). Transactions in turn consist of a number
of *exchanges* of different types. In particular, they begin and end with
boundary exchanges. Each different type of exchange has a structure
based on the types of *moves* made by the participants. For example, a
teacher-elicit exchange consists of an *initiating* move on the part of the
teacher, a *response* move from the student, and a *feedback* move from the
teacher. These moves may again be made up of a number of linguistic
acts. For example, a feedback move may consist of an *assessment*, an
evaluation, and a *comment*.

Sinclair and Coulthard's model of discourse structure appears to capture fairly well the normative structure of a particular type of formal
discourse. The basic framework (using five levels of discourse structure)
has been applied successfully to other types of discourse. For example,
Burton describes rules which capture the normal pattern of more informal discourse [Bur81], while Harris describes the structure of courtroom
discourse in similar terms [Har88]. Harris's approach is of interest as
it illustrates how the structure of different subtypes of discourse can
be represented. She showed that, while high level structure (sequences
of transactions) was fixed for a general discourse type (judicial court),
how these transactions were realized (in terms of allowed sequences of
exchanges) depended on the more specific discourse subtype.

There are problems with Sinclair and Coulthard's framework. For
example, in their model a type of category at one level in the model
(such as a type of exchange) may only be composed of categories in the
level below (such as a type of move). This appears overrestrictive, and
more recent models have generally used more flexible ways to describe
the options open to a participant in a discourse (e.g., [Car83, Rei81]).
However, the grammar is at least sufficiently clearly specified to be a
good basis for computational models of discourse, and variants of the
framework (e.g., [Bur81]) have been used in several dialogue systems
[FR86, Wac86, Bil91]. Our approach has therefore been to start with
this model, and extend and adapt it as needed. The rest of this section
will examine how far the explanatory dialogues in our corpus fit into the
basic framework.

Informing Transaction and Explanations   Sinclair and Coulthard
describe the structure of a number of different types of *transaction*.
These include the *directing* transaction, where the teacher instructs the

students to do some task, and the *informing* transaction, where the teacher informs the students about some topic. As might be expected, the explanatory dialogues analyzed fitted into Sinclair and Coulthard's definition of an informing transaction. We will therefore not be concerned with other types of transaction, or with higher levels of structure.

According to the model, an informing transaction starts and ends with a *boundary* exchange, with the body of the transaction consisting of an informing exchange, which may include within it different types of teaching exchange. Teaching exchanges include exchanges where the teacher asks a question of the students (*teacher-elicit* exchanges) and exchanges where a student asks a question of the teacher (*pupil-elicit* exchanges.

Although our dialogues could be viewed in these terms, there were a number of problems. First, it was clear that some boundary exchanges began major topics, while other boundary exchanges began subtopics within them. This suggests that we may have to describe a transaction on a major topic as consisting of a number of more fine-grained transactions on subtopics.

Second, the main body of a transaction appeared to be better viewed as a number of individual informing and teaching exchanges, rather than a single informing exchange with embedded teaching exchanges. An informing exchange could be viewed as an informing utterance and some opportunity for the explainee to indicate whether they were following. Given this definition, even monologue can be viewed as a sequence of informing exchanges, as a lack of interruption provides a kind of acknowledgment.

The next two sections will consider how far the structure of the different types of exchanges observed fit the model.

Boundary Exchanges   In Sinclair and Coulthard's model, an informing transaction is both opened and closed with a *boundary* exchange. The structure of these is given in figure 2.2.1 (where brackets indicate optional items). This definition is sufficiently flexible to allow a wide range of initial and final utterances (or none at all). All the initial exchanges in the circuit explanations fit this model,[7] but not the final

---

[7] Though there were frequently no verbal opening statements. This may have been influenced by the experimental situation where a third party set the topics to be discussed.

Boundary exchange: (frame move) (focusing move).

Frame move: marker.

Focussing move: (marker) (starter) meta-comment/conclusion.

Marker: discourse marker such as "OK," "Well."

Meta-comment: statement referring to future discourse.

Conclusion: statement referring to past discourse.

Starter: statement directing attention to a topic.

Figure 2.9
Sinclair and Coulthard's *Boundary* Exchange Structure

boundary exchanges.

Some opening statements are illustrated in figures 2.10 and 2.11. The first example (2.10) illustrates the use of meta-comments to open a topic, while the second illustrates the use of discourse markers. [8] Meta-comments were only occasionally used by the explainers, while discourse markers were fairly common.

The examples in figures 2.10 and 2.11 only include opening exchanges. In general there were less explicit indications of topic endings. However, figure 2.12 illustrates some examples of closing exchanges. (The complete explanations from which many of these extracts and examples were taken are given in appendix A.) The important thing about these is that (contrary to Sinclair and Coulthard's model) the final initiative is normally left with the novice. In many cases this was done using pauses in the conversation, though in the examples illustrated there were explicit checks or indications that the novice was happy and ready to continue to the next topic.

The form of the boundary exchange appeared to depend to some extent on the role adopted by the explainer. Explicit meta-comments were used more in the opening boundary exchange when a dominant tutorial role was adopted. The closing boundary exchange might be initiated by either the explainee or explainer, depending on who dominated the interaction.

---

[8] Meta-comments are comments which refer to the discourse itself, in this case to what is about to be said. Discourse markers are words like "Oh," "well," and "but" which indicate the structure and role of the discourse.

(1) What I'm going to do is to go through a set of circuits that I've got in front of me and I'm going to explain what the circuit does in a very general way and see if you can explain what happens when I change certain parameters. That way you'll be able to show your understanding of some simple circuits and some rather complex circuits.

(2) This is going to be a bit tricky and I'm going to get you to help me explain this one.

(3) What I'm going to do is to get you to explain this last circuit to me. Before I do that I better say briefly what a comparator is.

Figure 2.10
Opening Meta-Comments

(1) OK, Right, this is a circuit where the output is from a voltage divider.
(2) Well, it's a similar story here.
(3) OK, do you remember anything about transistors?
(4) OK, another one. So this is basically [...]
(5) OK, do you remember what this was.
(6) Now, there's various bits here.
(7) OK, so what's this going to do?
(8) OK, the lines are wires [...]
(9) Right, the next thing is analogous really.
(10) Right, now we get to the real fun, an inverter.
(11) Right, this thing is complicated.
(12) OK, well a comparator is fairly obvious.
(13) Right, low heat detector.

Figure 2.11
Discourse Markers on Topic Openings

---

(1) N: OK.
    E: Is that sufficient?
    N: I think I know what's going on with it.

(2) N: OK, that's just what I wanted to know to start with.
    E: OK?
    N: Yep.

(3) N: Yes, OK, I think I've got it.

(4) N: Alright.
    E: Enough of that one.

(5) N: That's enough of that one.

Figure 2.12
Closing Boundary Exchanges

As mentioned in the last section, boundary exchanges began both major topics and subtopics within them. Most of the examples given in figures 2.10–2.12 come at the beginning or end of an explanation of a particular circuit. However, the first meta-comment in figure 2.10 begins a whole session, explaining a whole set of circuits, while within a particular circuit explanation discourse markers (and occasionally meta-comments) were used to begin subtopics, such as describing a *component*, or starting the *process* explanation.

In conclusion then, Sinclair and Coulthard's notion of boundary exchanges at the beginning and end of topics seems to hold, though the detailed structure of these exchanges is different and depends on the roles adopted by the participants. In the circuit explanations analyzed, discourse markers and meta-comments are often used to open topics, and the ends of topics are negotiated. The closing boundary exchange does not fit in with Sinclair and Coulthard's model and corresponds more to the negotiations of ends of conversations discussed in [Lev83, ch6] for example. This may be due to the different roles of the participants, or due to the fact that the discourse is one-to-one.

Teacher-elicit exchange: initiating (eliciting) move, response move, feedback move.

Initiation move (eliciting): (marker) (starter) elicitation (prompt).

Response move: (acknowledge) reply (comment).

Feedback move: (accept) (evaluate) (comment).

Figure 2.13
Sinclair and Coulthard's *Teacher-Elicit* Exchange Structure

Teaching Exchanges   Having considered how topics are opened and closed, the next thing to consider is the structure of the exchanges within the topic. These include *teaching* exchanges and *informing* exchanges (though of course the informing exchanges may also be concerned with teaching). Teaching exchanges can be divided into *teacher-elicit* exchanges (using Sinclair and Coulthard's term), where the teacher asks the student(s) a question, and *pupil-elicit* exchanges, where the student asks the teacher a question. In tutorial discourse, where the roles of the participants are very different, the normal form of these two types of exchanges are also very different.

First, *teacher-elicit* exchanges will be considered. Sinclair and Coulthard suggest that in classroom discourse they consist of an initiating move by the teacher, a response move from the student, and some feedback by the teacher. The full definition is given in figure 2.13. This definition is sufficiently flexible to allow a range of detailed exchange structures. The only compulsory acts are the *elicitation* and the *reply*. However some exchanges still don't easily fit this pattern, so Sinclair and Coulthard extend the framework to allow *bound initiations* which serve both a feedback and initiation function. For example, the phrasing of a question may imply that the previous answer was correct or incorrect. This allows structures such as *initiation, response, bound-initiation, response, feedback*.

Figure 2.14 shows an exchange sequence from our corpus with its associated (possible) structure. However, even in this short example there appears to be some ambiguity in the analysis. For example, what exactly counts as a comment or a bound initiation? So, though it is possible to make this sequence fit Sinclair and Coulthard's model, that may not be saying very much. Overall, while the model is useful in suggesting some

Utterance	Classification
E: So what will be the voltage here?	Initiation (elicitation)
N: 9V?	Response (reply)
E: It will be closer to 9V, that's right.	Feedback (comment?, accept)
E: And if there isn't any light on it?	Initiation (elicitation)
N: It will consume, I don't know how much.	Response (reply)
E: OK, If no light falls on it then the resistance?	Bound initiation (marker, elicitation)
N: Will be high, and will not let through current.	Response (reply)
E: So the voltage here will be?	Bound Initiation (elicitation)
N: Tending to zero.	Response (reply)
E: Closer to nought.	Feedback (accept)

Figure 2.14
Example Teaching Exchanges

of the moves and acts which might be included in exchanges, some of the details appear somewhat ill-defined.

One problem with the simple model of teaching exchanges proposed by Sinclair and Coulthard is that it doesn't allow feedback "moves" themselves to involve new exchanges. Yet a teacher will frequently respond to a student's error by initiating a remedial subdialogue (as in utterances 5–10 in figure 2.14). The whole subdialogue has the function of providing feedback to the student, so we should extend the model to allow such complex feedback moves (rather than treating them as *bound initiations* as described above). The content of these "moves" will be discussed in section 2.3 when we examine work on remedial strategies in tutorial dialogues.

The second type of teaching exchange is the *pupil-elicit* exchange, which involves the student questioning the teacher. According to Sinclair and Coulthard, this has similar structure to the *teacher-elicit* exchange, but without the feedback move — a student is not normally expected to comment on a teacher's answer to a question.

However, again, this type of analysis fails to capture the fact that student questions may initiate long and complex explanations involving more exchanges. It seems vital to be able to treat these complex answers as responses, while allowing for exchanges within the response. Consider

N: What are the components in that circuit?
E: Right, that one is a variable resistor, Its resistance can be set by that knob.
    N: What's the difference between this variable resistor and the one
    in circuit B, because they have different diagrams.
    E: There is a resistor between here, and this point is in contact withE:
    [...] (clarification)
    N: Right.
This is an OPAMP, a feature of which is, well it has two significant features.
    E: One is that the inputs make very little [...]
        N: I don't understand.
        E: This circuit, this wire here [...] (long clarification)
        So if the resistor here is set with the two halves equal then
        the voltage will be exactly half way between the two, so it
        doesn't make any difference, and similarly this one here has
        no effect, very small amounts come in.
    E: The other thing that it does is amplify [...]

Figure 2.15
Complex Replies and Resumptions

the example given in figure 2.15 (indented according to illustrate the discourse structure). In this case the expert's response to the initial question goes on for several pages (or minutes), involving many further exchanges.

The example in figure 2.15 also illustrates clearly how interruptions may be "put on a stack," and the previous discourse resumed once the query has been dealt with. Such resumptions are sometimes marked with discourse markers such as "anyway," particularly if the interruption was on a different topic. In the example explanations, such discourse markers were occasionally used, but not consistently. More often, pauses are used to mark the discourse structure. Sinclair and Coulthard's model does not consider how interruptions are incorporated in the discourse structure, and should be extended to accommodate them.

Informing Exchanges In Sinclair and Coulthard's model, the other main type of exchange considered is the informing exchange. This involves an informing statement by the teacher, and optional acknowledgment from the student(s). The informing statement could involve an arbitrary number of utterances.

In the explanatory dialogues analyzed here, informing statements came from both expert and novice, and they were frequently followed by corrections or follow-up comments. Within an informing section, pauses and gestures could be used to provide acknowledgments. If the novice had an opportunity to interrupt to indicate they weren't following, and failed to take up that opportunity, this too could be viewed as an implicit acknowledgement. In this view then, each informing statement where the other participant has the opportunity to interrupt is viewed as an informing exchange, whether or not the other participant responds.

In human discourse a speaker may give the other participant the opportunity to interrupt without even pausing. These possible interruption points are sometimes referred to as *transition relevance points* [SSJ78]. Such points frequently occur at sentence boundaries, though other basic turn units (or *turn constructional units*) are possible. However, for interactive explanations involving a computer (using written textual interaction) larger units are more likely to be appropriate. The system may have to explicitly pause and require the user at least to press a key or click a button before it continues. Where there is low risk of confusion then it may be best to present a whole page before pausing. These issues will be referred to again in chapter 4.

Other Exchange Types? There are two other types of exchange observed in the corpus which were not part of Sinclair and Coulthard's definition of an informing transaction. First there are cases where the expert or the novice gives a direction or request concerning the way the explanation should progress. The other participant typically then acknowledges, and adjusts their behavior. Example requests (from the novice) include:

(1) Why don't you write down formulas so we can see what's going on.
(2) I need to know what's the point of this particular bit, rather than an explanation at a lower level.

The second type of exchange consists of a question from the expert concerning whether or not the novice knows some concept, and an answer from the novice. Example questions include:

(1) First of all, do you remember from physics what these things do?
(2) Have you got the hang of these potential dividers yet?

The above type of exchange is vital both in order to tailor explanations to the user's level of understanding, and to check that some explanation has been understood. It is useful to distinguish them from cases where the teacher (or explainer) is *testing* the user's knowledge, as in the examples in figure 2.14.

Conclusion The above discussion has been fairly informal, using illustrative examples to show where Sinclair and Coulthard's framework needs to be adapted to be useful as the basis for a computational model of explanatory discourse. (The corpus isn't large enough for more quantitative results to be meaningful.) The following adaptations appear necessary:

- If discourse *moves* are defined functionally (such as *response* or *feedback*) then they must be allowed to span a whole section of discourse, perhaps involving further exchanges.
- A wider range of exchange types were used in this slightly less formal type of tutorial discourse. Each of these must be defined.
- It appears useful to view an informing statement where the student has the opportunity to interrupt as an informing exchange, with an implicit acknowledgment. This avoids lengthy monologues being viewed as a single undifferentiated informing move.
- The model should be extended to deal with interruptions. The structure of an interruption can be characteristically defined in terms of an opening discourse marker, interrupting text and a closing marker (e.g., "anyway") and repetition or meta-comment to resume.

It is perhaps not surprising that the model needs considerable modification in order to capture useful features of the discourse. It was designed to capture the characteristic structure of teacher-student interaction, and not for the computational modeling of explanatory discourse. Nevertheless it has proved a useful basic framework, and easy to extend in the directions indicated.

2.2.2   Participant Roles and Discourse Structure

Although all of the dialogues analyzed could be fitted into the same basic framework, discussed above, they varied widely in style. These different dialogue styles appeared to be influenced by the roles adopted by the participants. This included who had the dominant role in the interaction (if any), and who was responsible for ensuring that the explanation was understood. The different styles observed are summarized below, and illustrated in figures 2.16–2.20. Each of the five dialogues illustrated was generated by a different expert-novice pair. The dialogue styles were:

Expert-dominant-informing: The expert dominates the explanation, but does not check on the novice's understanding or initiate teaching exchanges. The novice interrupts with clarification questions when confused, but these do not dominate the interaction.

Novice-dominant-informing: As above, but the questions asked by the novice dominate the whole course of the interaction.

Expert-dominant-tutorial: The expert adopts the dominant role, leading the novice through the explanation, checking their understanding as the explanation progresses.

Novice-dominant-tutorial: The novice dominates the dialogue by asking questions and proposing steps in the explanation, but the expert observes and corrects the novice when incorrect.

Cooperative-informing: Expert and novice contribute equally to the explanation, each contributing steps and possibly querying the other.

The example in figure 2.16 illustrates an explanation largely dominated by the expert. Clarification questions from the novice are answered, but are treated as interruptions. Note that the expert's third utterance starts with a discourse marker ("well") and is essentially a repeat of part of the first utterance. This is a common technique for resuming an explanation, following an interruption.

Figure 2.17 shows how follow-up questions asked by the novice can dominate the interaction. In the full example there were 15 question-answer pairs initiated by the novice, making up the bulk of the dialogue.

In these first two example dialogues, it is the expert explaining, and the novice asking questions. Figures 2.18 and 2.19 illustrate two types of dialogue where the novice contributes many of the steps of the explanation. In the first (figure 2.18) the novice is leading the explanation, but the expert is following and commenting on the novice's contributions. In the second (figure 2.19) the expert is explicitly leading the novice through the steps of the explanation, dominating the dialogue but again

E: These components here, you might consider them as being both resistors. Two variable resistors. I can write down a relation for resistance..

N: You'll have to tell me what a resistance is.

E: A resistor is just [...] (clarification subdialogue)

N: I see, or at least, I think I see.

E: Well, in this circuit here there are just two resistors, switched in serial mode. You can think of it as one resistor supplied with a voltage 9V, and there will be a current flowing through the circuit. Well, the output can be calculated by, when you know the current flowing here then you can assume that the output doesn't take any current, so the current here is nil. The output voltage is determined by this current multiplied by this resistance. In order to calculate the current you have to include this resistor in your network as well,

N: Why are we bothered about what the current through there is. What's going to happen, I have to know the purpose of it.

E: In the end you want to know this voltage [...]

N: OK

E: I can just write down a relationship, this is I1 [...]

Figure 2.16
Expert-dominant-informing Dialogue (Light Detector)

E: In this circuit we have an output whose voltage depends on the amount of light falling on the LDR. And the more light falls on here, the more it will conduct so the higher the voltage will be here.

N: What does LDR stand for?

E: Light-dependent resistor.

N: What's this bit?

E: That's a variable resistor, so you can change how the output level varies with the resistance of the LDR.
[...]

Figure 2.17
Novice-dominant-informing Dialogue (Light Detector)

E: Right, the next thing is exactly analogous really.

N: OK, what's this?

E: That means it's a variable resistor [...]
Right, the heat detector unit is exactly analogous in fact. How do you think it works?

N: Right, presumably depending on the amount of heat here, if it has, the more heat it has the more resistance it has?

E: Probably the less.

N: The less heat it has the more resistance it has?

E: Sorry, no, the hotter it is the less resistance.

N: The hotter it is the less resistance. So, if it's not hot at all, if it's cold, if it's very high resistance therefore this middle one is closer to zero, and if it's very very hot it has low resistance so it's closer to 9V here.
But I don't see what difference this 5K or 10K makes?
[...]

Figure 2.18
Novice-dominant-tutorial Dialogue (Heat Detector)

checking carefully on what the novice understands and correcting any misunderstandings.

The final example (figure 2.20) illustrates a dialogue where the expert-novice roles are less well defined, and neither participant dominates the interaction. In this case each participant is trying to understand how the circuit works, suggesting to the other what might happen. It is unclear how far the participants are checking on the other's understanding.

In principle we would like our model of explanatory discourse to be able to accommodate all these different dialogue styles, involving a wide range of types of exchanges between expert and novice. However, to simplify things the EDGE system does not allow the user to initiate *informing* exchanges. If we didn't place this restriction it would be necessary to try and make sense of the user's attempts at explanation, and work out appropriate responses and continuations based on this. This is beyond the scope of the current work, but remains an important direction for further work.

E: OK, do you remember anything about transistors? Basically, the important thing about transistors is [...] so the current going through the collector and emitter

N: Is amplified.

E: is 100 or 200 times bigger than the current going through here. The arrow here just tells you which way you should connect it.
Right, so what's going to happen here, say if you consider this as an input and this as an output, what happens when you make this voltage high, what happens to this?

N: When you make it high you probably get all the current from this end amplified.

E: Well, when you make the current high

N: It opens the gate.

E: Yeah, what's going to happen to the resistance between here and here?

N: It's going to be low.

E: So what's going to happen to the voltage here, if you have a very low resistance?

N: It's going to tend to a high limit.

E: Careful. If you let the current through these two then it's just as if you wired these two up, a little bit. So it's just as if the transistor weren't there and these two were connected. So if these two are connected there's nothing here in fact, so what's the voltage here going to be?

N: Well, the same voltage as the other end.

E: Yes, so it's going to be low.
[...]

Figure 2.19
Expert-dominant-tutorial Dialogue (Inverter)

N: [...] It would be an inverter if there was a wire coming out here.

E: Oh, right, but we'll have, that would be raised to zero volts.

N: Right, if there is light shining on this, the resistance goes down, which means that this will get to 9, and that's already 9, so this will be zero, that will be zero and because we have a zero here this is..

E: Up there, that thing up there.

N: We have a zero on the first one.

E: Well, the first one will be going from zero to one all the time.

N: So, looking at the table, that point there, for this whole inverter will be going 1-1, so it will always be on..
(Experimenter clarification)
So we've got 1, so this is always going to be at 9, so there's always a voltage across there,

E: So it's not going to produce a sound, so this is one where if you break the light then it will..

N: So that's going to happen in that case [...] so this will be varying between 9 and 0 so will be going nee naw nee naw.

Figure 2.20
Cooperative-informing Dialogue (Burglar Alarm)

2.3   The Relation between Content Organization and Dialogue Structure

So far in this chapter we have looked at the structure of the content of an explanation, and the structure of the dialogue between expert and novice. However, if we are to develop an integrated model of explanatory dialogues which takes into account both the content and the interactions then we need to look at the relation between the two.

As mentioned in section 2.1, it was sometimes hard to analyze the organization of the content of the dialogues because user interruptions and follow-up questions dominated the dialogue. However, all the dialogues appeared to follow the same basic pattern. The dialogues could be viewed as a main explanation, where the content of the interactions basically followed the content grammar given in section 2.1, plus a number of follow-up exchanges, where the novice asked further questions to fill in gaps in their knowledge. The main explanation could be interrupted by clarification questions, which might result in lengthy clarification subdialogues, but would normally be resumed at the end of the interruption. Steps of the main explanation could be contributed by either the novice, the expert, or via an exchange involving both.

In figures 2.16–2.20 we can see how the content of the dialogues follows the basic content grammar. For example, in figure 2.17 the initial sequence of statements from the expert follows a basic *function-process* pattern, with follow-up questions largely addressing background information that was missed out of this short explanation. In figure 2.16 the "main" explanation follows the *constituency-process* pattern, though this is interrupted by questions from the novice (again addressing missing background knowledge). In this example though, the *process* description is given in terms of circuit equations. Finally figure 2.18 illustrates a dialogue where the content follows the same *constituency-process* patten, but some of the steps are contributed jointly by the expert and the novice.

This observed relation between dialogue structure and content structure is analogous to the relation between dialogue structure and task structure in task-oriented dialogues [Gro77]. In this case the task is to convey some complex concepts to the novice, and the content of the dialogue reflects this task. Of course, just because the content follows a given pattern does not mean that the details are determined in ad-

vance. The expert will respond to the novice's confusions and adjust the
level at which an explanation is given (for example, giving more or less
background information) depending on the interactions with the novice.
Local coherence may also influence the detailed planning of the explanation. Gilbert, for example, analyzed advisory dialogues where neither
expert nor novice dominated the interaction and suggested that after
each utterance by the advisee, the advisor seeks to find a partial plan
which is coherent with the last utterance, yet contributes to the overall goal of the conversation [Gil87]. This appears to be a valid model
for the dialogues analyzed and is consistent with the EDGE approach,
discussed in the next chapters.

In order to account fully for the content of the explanatory dialogues
it was necessary to extend slightly the content grammar given in section 2.1, and add a component to the model to deal with the content of
tutorial responses (remediation). The content grammar was extended
to allow more complex constituency and process descriptions, such as
allowing additional circuit or component attributes to be mentioned in
both these parts of the explanation. These extensions are largely consistent with McKeown's and Paris's schemata.

Dealing with remedial responses was slightly more complex. There
has been a large amount of work on tutorial dialogues within the field
of intelligent tutoring systems (surveyed in [Wen87] for example). Much
of this work has been concerned with how teachers react to student errors and misconceptions and provide responses which enable students
to understand their mistakes. The WHY project, for example, analyzed the strategies used by teachers who used the "Socratic" approach
to teaching [CS82]. When a student got an answer wrong, a limited
number of strategies could be used to lead the student to understand
their misconception and work out the correct answer. Woolf and Murray
suggested that schemata could be used to capture common remediation
strategies [WM87]. In their remediation schema there should be some
"grain of truth acknowledgment" followed by one of three types of remediation depending on the type of error. These types of remediation
involve teaching the students the *consequence* of their incorrect answer,
or giving *examples* or *guidance* leading the student toward the correct
answer.

In the *expert-dominant-tutorial* style explanatory dialogues, similar
strategies were observed. One of these dialogue sections was illustrated

in figure 2.19 (with the complete explanation in appendix A) and another is given in figure 2.21 along with comments suggesting the basic strategies that appear to be being used.

In figure 2.21 two strategies are apparent. If a question is answered with a contributing step (rather than the final answer) then the expert acknowledges that step and prompts for further steps. If the answer to the original question is incorrect or confused, then the expert may use the strategy of prompting for substeps to lead the novice to understand the answer. Another strategy seen in figure 2.19 is to supply supplementary information (such as substeps or an analogy) and then ask the question again.

The strategies chosen may depend on the type of question asked, on what the user knows, and on the particular pedagogical or dialogue strategy being pursued. Our model of explanatory discourse allows such strategies to be defined and selected, but does not attempt to enumerate a wide range of such strategies.

2.4 Toward a Computational Model of Explanatory Discourse

The details of the computational model developed for modeling these kinds of explanatory dialogues will be developed over the remainder of the book. However, we will outline the basic approach here and show how further details of the dialogues analyzed, such as the use of discourse markers and pronouns, fit into the model.

In section 2.1 we showed how the content of the explanations could be explained in terms of plans, using prerequisite and subskill relations, while in section 2.2 we showed that a hierarchical model of dialogue structure could form a useful basis for modeling the organization of the interactions. The EDGE model uses simple content and dialogue planning rules to capture both these aspects of discourse structure. At the top level a *transaction* dialogue planning rule describes how an explanation consists of an opening boundary exchange, a sequence of teaching exchanges, and a closing boundary exchange. However, the content of the teaching exchanges is determined by the content planning rules, so control soon switches to content planning. Each unit of content (i.e., proposition) may be conveyed either by an *informing* exchange or a

Utterance	Comment
E: What's going to happen to the voltage here, depending on whether the light falls on it or not?	
N: When the light falls the resistance will be, uh..	Contributes part of a step toward the answer.
E: The resistance will be low.	Provides answer to that step.
N: So all the current will go through.	Provides next step and pauses.
E: OK, so there will be more current going through, so what will be the voltage here?	Prompts for next step in argument and hence answer to original question.
N: 9V?	Provides answer (or very close).
E: It will be closer to 9V, that's right. And if there isn't any light on it?	Response and new question.
N: It will consume, I don't know how much.	Unhelpful answer/step.
E: OK, if no light falls on it then the resistance?	Simpler question leading to answer.
N: Will be high, and will not let through current.	Two correct steps.
E: So the voltage here will be?	So next question leads to answer to original question.
N: Tending to zero.	Correct answer (but perhaps badly phrased).
E: Closer to nought.	Rephrase answer.

Figure 2.21
Commented Tutorial Dialogue Fragment

teacher-elicit exchange, and dialogue planning rules are again used to select the exchange type and determine its structure.

User initiative is restricted to asking questions. These can interrupt the main flow of the explanation, or come after the main explanation. If they interrupt the explanation then they may influence the remaining explanation.

The basic model is clearly plan-based (though the dialogue planning rules are very simple). There is a fairly well defined *intentional structure* [GS86]. (The relevant intentions are to make some topic or subtopic understood by the hearer.) *Dominance* relations occur between goals and subgoals in the content plans, while *satisfaction precedence* relations occur between prerequisite goals and subgoals in content plans. Grosz and Sidner suggest that the discourse segmentation and focus is closely related to the intentional structure. In turn, discourse markers and the use of referring expressions relate to the discourse segmentation and focus space. This suggests that we may find corroboration for our model in the form of discourse markers and pronoun use in the dialogues analyzed.

Consider for example the use of pronouns in figure 2.15. In the last line "it" refers to the operational amplifier and not to the resistor mentioned in the previous utterance. This is consistent with the discourse segmentation indicated (by indentation) given Grosz and Sidner's theory of discourse structure.

We have already noted how topics frequently begin with a discourse marker (such as "OK"). In some cases, subtopics are also signaled in this way. One expert for example, in a long explanation, signaled the start of the whole explanation with "OK," and the start of the *process* section with "Right." Another speaker started the explanation with a meta-comment, and used markers to indicate the beginnings of the *function* and *process* descriptions. This suggests that the basic goal-subgoal structure developed is reasonable, though the results are by no means conclusive.

Of course, the model of dialogue structure outlined above has a number of limitations. In particular, it does not provide a sufficiently general and flexible model, being based on a discourse grammar, abstracted from the analysis of a specific type of dialogue. We have not fully demonstrated *why*, for example, closing boundary exchanges of particular forms occur in tutorial or explanatory dialogues. The result is a practical model that can be applied given a restricted type of dialogue, but not a general model that can easily be extended and adapted to generate and make sense of all types of dialogues. "Intention-based" models of dialogue (discussed in chapter 4) may provide a better basis. However, developing such intention-based models for cooperative dialogues is still a hard problem, with much ongoing research, mostly theoretically oriented (e.g., in [CMP90]). At this point it appears more practical to base practical systems at least partially on normative models, influenced in part by these more theoretical intention-based models. Developing practical systems based on more general models of dialogue will be left to further research.

2.5   Conclusion

In this chapter we have described the analysis of a small corpus of explanations concerning how circuits work, and derived the structure both of the content of the explanations and of the interactions between explainer and explainee. The content structure can be described using a content grammar or schema similar to those used by McKeown and Paris [McK85, Par88] while the dialogue structure can be described using a discourse grammar adapted from work on tutorial dialogues [SC75]. The content of interactive explanations appears to follow the same basic patterns as the content of uninterrupted explanations, apart from interruptions from the explainee and remedial responses from the explainer given some apparent misunderstanding.

We have suggested how the details of the content might depend on assumptions about the explainee's knowledge, and details of the dialogue depend on the roles and responsibilities of the participants. These suggestions are only hypotheses — it is not possible to determine the basis on which these choices are made solely from the transcripts. However, the proposals begin to provide a framework for explaining the structure of the observed dialogues. This allows us both to generalize the results more easily and to better generate explanatory dialogues which depend on the discourse situation. Choices in the dialogue can be explained in terms of a simple planning process, with actions selected depending on the hearer's knowledge and the roles of the participants.

There are a number of problems with the analysis because of the mode of interaction (face-to-face, verbal) and the minimal transcription (pauses and intonation were not transcribed). It is difficult to know what role intonational cues, for example, may play in helping the explainee to make sense of the explanation, and how results based on verbal discourse can be applied to a text-based explanation generation system. Physical actions by the explainer (such as pointing and sketching) were not transcribed, though it was often clear where they had been used. Again, it is unclear whether such actions should be used in text-based interaction in the same way as in verbal interaction.

Another issue is the unnaturalness of the experiment, compared with a realistic explanation situation. The experts were given a definite goal (to explain how a set of eight circuits worked) and particular materials (a set of circuit diagrams and a pencil). This allowed us to determine the structure of explanations given this particular goal, but may miss important information about how people explain in *context*, given an information need in a particular real situation.

Despite these problems, the analysis revealed useful insights about explanatory dialogues, which could be used in the development of a computational model. The remainder of this book will be concerned with this computational model.

3 Planning Explanation Content

In the following four chapters we will show how an interactive explanation may be generated given some topic to be explained. This involves deciding what to say in an explanation, deciding how to manage the dialogue, and deciding how to update assumptions about the user's knowledge (using these to influence the developing explanation).

In this chapter we will consider how a system can decide on the content of an explanation given assumptions about the user's knowledge. The content should be chosen and structured in such a way that the hearer can easily assimilate the new knowledge. For example, the following explanation fragment (discussed in chapter 2) will only fully make sense if the user is familiar with what a potential divider circuit is, and with what a light dependent resistor and a variable resistor are:

"Well, this here looks to be a potential divider circuit, and it contains two components one of which is a light dependent resistor and the other is a variable resistor."

If the necessary background concepts are not understood by the user then either they should be explained or the circuit should be described in another way that does not make use of the unknown concepts. For example, if the user did not know what a potential divider circuit was the following (made up) description might make more sense:

"This is a circuit which is used to provide a varying output voltage depending on the values of these two resistors. One of the resistors is a light dependent resistor, and the other an ordinary variable resistor."

The first two sections of this chapter present some of the problems and issues involved in generating multi-sentence texts in general. We consider some of the different principles that govern the structure and content of a text, and discuss the problem of text planning, where a system must decide on that structure and content given a communicative goal.

The remainder of the chapter looks at the particular problem of explanation planning, first considering the general principles that should guide the construction of an explanation, and then presenting the EDGE explanation content planner. This component forms part of the overall

EDGE system, illustrated earlier in figure 1.1. In particular the content planning rules and discourse planner are introduced.

3.1 Principles Governing the Structure and Content of Texts

Before developing a text planning system it is helpful to consider what general principles govern the structure and content of a text, and which ones are the most important for a particular application. We can then focus on the most important issues, while remaining aware of issues which remain to be addressed if an application-independent text planning architecture is to be developed.

In the rest of this section we therefore discuss a number of principles governing text structure. The first seven of these are based on work in text linguistics, which is concerned with how texts function in human interaction [dBD81]. De Beaugrande and Dressler proposed seven standards of *textuality* which provide a general set of principles which should guide the construction of texts. These principles are closely interrelated, but provide different perspectives on the organization and content of texts. The last principle is an additional one relating to the use of extralinguistic devices within a text.[1]

Cohesion: Surface Level Ties The first principle relates to the surface organization of text. Cohesive relationships are surface level ties between elements in a text, and have been discussed in detail by Halliday and Hasan [HH76], for example. Devices which aid the cohesion of a text include pronouns, appropriate conjunctions, lexical and syntactic repetition, and ellipsis.

These devices are clearly important, enabling economy of presentation while allowing the reader to make appropriate links between successive sentences. While recognizing its importance, this book does not address such aspects of surface expression, concentrating on the structure of the overall discourse. However, if text is to be readable, certain aspects cannot be ignored, as the cohesive devices used may influence the way a discourse is interpreted. The most important of these is perhaps the use of pronouns. For example, the following examples of two consecutive

---

[1]We will use the term "text" in this chapter to include non-interactive spoken discourse, and will use the terms reader/writer and speaker/hearer interchangeably.

sentences seem very unnatural:

1. The light detector unit is a kind of potential divider circuit.
2. The light detector unit's function is to provide an output voltage which depends on the input light intensity.

1. Today we are going to make chocolate chip cookies.
2. Do you know how to make chocolate chip cookies?

The repetition of noun phrase and verb phrase respectively not only makes for uneconomical presentation, but destroys the structure of the discourse, encouraging the hearer to believe that the second sentence begins a new topic. The appropriate use of pronouns will therefore be considered essential to the generation of explanatory text and should be used even in a simplistic treatment of sentence level generation.

Coherence: Conceptual Relations   The term *coherence* will here be used to refer to the relations between the concepts or ideas expressed in different parts of a text. A coherent text is one where the conceptual relations underlying a surface text are accessible to the reader. These relations may be implicit, and only accessible by inference using commonsense and specific knowledge. For example, the utterance:

"Let's go for a pizza. Muck's gone down."

would not seem coherent to someone who didn't realize that the speaker was the user of a computer called Muck (named after the Scottish island), who had nothing to do while his computer was down. Of course, if this background information was known to the hearer then including it would appear verbose and unnatural.

So, whether they are explicit or not, there should be relations between the concepts underlying a text. These may describe links between the objects and actions mentioned in each utterance, or between the ideas expressed in whole sections of text. Links between objects and actions have been discussed in terms of rules governing *focus* movement (e.g., [MC91, McK85]), while links between ideas in (and roles of) whole sections have been discussed in terms of sets of *rhetorical relations* which can apply between sections of a text (e.g., [Hob83, MT87a]).

Intentionality: The Speaker's Goal An acceptable text (from the writer's point of view) is one that achieves the writer's goals. In a sense, this principle subsumes the others as the overriding principle governing text content and structure. A text will only achieve its goals if it is well-formed in all respects. However, there are aspects of text structure which are directly related to the writer's goals and intentions. Grosz and Sidner claim that the structure of a text is based on the relations between the intentions of the speaker or writer [GS86], and in particular on *dominance* relations and *satisfaction precedence* relations. Each subsection of a text may achieve a distinct purpose, each of which contributes to the overall purpose of the text.

If the reader is expected to recognize the intentions behind a section of text then it may be helpful to give *meta-comments* describing what a section of a text is being used to achieve. For example, a section of a paper may begin with an utterance like the following:

"In this section we will demonstrate that text planning is a complex and ill-understood area."

For a text to satisfy our principle of intentionality it should be rationally planned to satisfy the goals of the speaker,[2] and these goals should be recognizable by the reader if this is appropriate.

Acceptability: The Hearer's Goals and Attitudes The acceptability principle relates to the hearer's attitude to the text. If textual communication is to succeed, then the hearer must recognize the text as relevant to their goals and interests. For example, a scientific paper will not be effective if it is not relevant to the interests of its readership, while an instructional text will not be effective if it is not deemed relevant by the student.

Informativity: The Hearer's Knowledge A text should be sufficiently informative, without overloading the hearer. Even if a piece

---

[2]There is some dispute about how far people do "rationally plan out" their discourse [Suc87, Sib91]. Many would claim that discourse results from many local decisions made on the basis of the immediate situation which is not or cannot be predicted in advance, not from prior plans to achieve high level goals. We suggest that both local decisions and overall goals are important. In some kinds of discourse (such as everyday conversations, or informal descriptions of events) local decisions are dominant, while in other kinds of discourse the speaker has well defined goals which must be planned for and satisfied.

of text addresses the goals and interests of the reader, it may fail to
be effective if too much or too little new information is given, of if the
information cannot be easily linked in with the reader's existing knowledge. In general then, generating an informative text should involve
finding links between the *target* information to be communicated, and
the reader's existing knowledge. This can be done either by selecting a
particular way to communicate the target information which relates well
to the existing knowledge, or by explaining background material which
provides the necessary connecting links. For example, when explaining
how a circuit works to someone unfamiliar with the concept of resistance
it might be possible to think of a way of explaining that does not use
that unknown concept, relating only to existing knowledge. However,
another strategy would be to explain resistance first, thus making a link
between future references to resistance and the reader's prior knowledge.

Situationality: The Discourse Context De Beaugrande's sixth
standard of textuality concerns the factors that make a text relevant
to its situation of occurrence. The discourse situation includes both the
prior discourse and the wider discourse situation. The prior discourse
constrains how it may develop, as each utterance creates and extends
the context within which all later utterances must make sense.

The wider discourse situation includes things like the current activities
of the participants, the mode of interaction (e.g., face-to-face verbal),
and the roles of the participants. The term *discourse register* is often
used to denote the set of factors which represent this wider discourse
context [HH89].

Many of the other principles can be viewed in terms of the way they
make the discourse appropriate to the situation. The use of coherence
and cohesive relations depends on the prior text, while the participants'
goals, knowledge, and attitudes can be viewed as aspects of the wider
discourse situation.

Conventionality There are many conventions governing the way a
text is constructed which may be hard to trace back to the more general
principles described above. For example, a business letter has a standard form which has evolved and crystalized over time. All texts have
some element of conventional form. When reading or writing a text we
make use of our knowledge of other texts of the same type. When writing we can use the established normal text form to straightforwardly

create an appropriate text, and when making sense of a text there may
be convention-based expectations about what will follow which will help
us in our interpretation. The conventions may have originally resulted
from a consideration of the speaker's intentions, the audience, the discourse situation, and general rules of discourse coherence. However, the
establishment of stereotypical text forms allows us to write and make
sense of a text more efficiently. Where the conventional form is strongly
established it is impossible to make sense of or generate a text without
knowledge of the conventions.

In general, generating a text will involve both making use of the conventional structures known to be relevant for that particular text type,
and planning to meet new goals, situations, and hearers [CC77, pg 236].
Unusual situations and difficult goals will require more active planning,
while common situations may require little thought, using preexisting
schemata. As writers become more expert, certain types of discourse
become "compiled" and can be followed more or less automatically.

Textual conventions may relate both to the subject matter of the
text and to the type of the text. Kieras distinguishes between *content
schemata* and *text grammars* [Kie85]. The former refer to stereotypical patterns used for arranging the content (facts) in different domains,
while the latter refer to more domain independent configurations of textual elements which may be influenced by the type of text (such as an
instructional text).

Content schemata of various kinds have been discussed by many researchers (e.g., [Rum75, McK85]), although there is some dispute concerning how far they may be explained by more general principles. For
example, stories appear to have a conventional structure [Rum75, MJ80],
yet this structure can arguably be explained in terms of a representation
of the goals and plans of the participants in the story [BW79].

Text grammars (as we are using the term here) refer to the conventional organization of a text independent of what is conveyed in that
text. A text consists of much more than an arrangement of facts or
propositions. Summaries, introductions, headers, and different types of
meta-comments and discourse markers are used to increase the effectiveness of the text. These are used in a conventional manner which
depends on the type of the text. For example, in educational discourse
meta-comments of different types are used frequently, sometimes representing the majority of utterances [Stu76, SC75]. In newspaper articles,

headers, leads, and summaries are again used in a characteristic manner [vD85]. Both meta-comments and headlines make it easier for the reader or hearer to make sense of the text, serving as "advance organizers," directing the reader to the relevant knowledge.

Extralinguistic Devices   The final principle governing text content and structure concerns the use of extralinguistic devices such as diagrams and pointing actions. The use of diagrams and graphical actions is clearly not necessary for all types of texts. However, for certain kind of explanations (such as explaining how to get somewhere, or how a physical device works) the use of diagrams is very important. There has been increasing interest in the last few years on the problem of generating appropriate multimedia explanations. The appropriate combination of text with other media is therefore added as an important principle for the generation of effective texts.

3.2   The Problem of Text Planning

The principles described above relate to the factors which influence the structure and content of a text. A text should be generated which is appropriate given:

- The speaker's (or writer's) goal.
- The hearer's (or audience's) goals, knowledge, and preferences.
- Any conventions governing texts of the particular text type concerned.
- Any preceding text, and other aspects of the discourse situation.

The text should depend on the above factors while conforming to general principles governing textual cohesion and coherence. Changing any one of the factors above should potentially change the preferred structure and content of the text. Each of the factors listed above may be viewed as a feature of the general discourse situation in which the text is constructed. A particular text type may be defined in terms of the sets of texts appropriate given some restricted set of these features.

The basic problem in text planning is how to generate a coherent, appropriate multi-sentence text given knowledge of the discourse situation. A flexible generation system should be able to make a number of different choices concerning the structure and content of the text, where each choice depends on one or more aspects of the discourse situation.

The simplest possible way of achieving this is to create by hand a different text for every possible situation (or at least, for every situation that we want to distinguish). This is referred to as the *canned text* approach. For example, suppose we wanted a system that could generate (or rather, select) appropriate texts given knowledge of seven types of question that could be asked by any of three classes of user about ten objects in the domain. The question answerer's goals would be related to the question type and the domain object, so there could be 70 distinct speaker goals. If an appropriate text were to be generated for each class of user then 210 texts would have to be constructed by hand. It should be clear that this approach soon becomes impracticable. For a moderately complex documentation system it has been suggested that hundreds of thousands of canned texts would be required, even if only faily simple tailoring to the user is attempted [RML92]. And if we wanted to extend such a system to take into account further aspects of the discourse situation (such as a new class of user) then a whole batch of new texts would have to be written.

So, text planning is concerned with ways of creating appropriate, coherent texts without this enormous overhead. Early work started with the recognition that texts of certain types have common basic patterns of organization [Wei80, McK85]. For example, descriptions of objects follow certain common patterns, independent of the object being described. One such pattern (mentioned in chapters 1 and 2) is to present the constituents of the object being described, present characteristic information about each constituent in turn, and then present additional characteristic information about the object [McK85]. By analyzing texts of a particular type it is possible to abstract these common patterns, and use them in order to generate coherent descriptions of a whole range of different objects.

At their very simplest, these text patterns could be simply templates, to be filled in with the attributes of the object being described. This is possible if all the objects to be described share the same attributes, and can be described in the same manner. However, if we want to avoid this restriction and to attempt to capture the range of descriptions generated by humans, then more flexible patterns (or *schemata*) must be used [McK85, Par87, Par88]. These effectively provide a range of choices that can be followed when constructing a certain type of text (see section 2.1). The features of the object being described can then influence the choices made, while remaining choices can be made on the basis of *focus* rules, which provide a set of preferences concerning the way new focused objects may be introduced in the text.

The schema-based approach can be extended to allow texts to be generated which depend on particular aspects of the discourse situation (i.e., for more detailed text types). For example, by analyzing descriptions aimed at experts and descriptions aimed at relative novices Paris was able to obtain distinct schemata for each type of text [Par88]. By using these different schemata in conjunction, her generation system could give descriptions which were appropriately tailored given knowledge of whether the user had expertise concerning the different subparts of an object being described.

Using schemata provides us with a fairly practical and effective way of generating coherent descriptions given objects to be described. Different schemata may be used for different types of text, so as long as we are essentially only concerned with a small range of text types there isn't too much overhead. However, if we want to generate texts which depend on further and more detailed aspects of the discourse situation then the approach appears to suffer from the same problems as the canned text approach described first. In order to generate texts to answer seven types of question, addressed to three classes of user, we might in principle want to create up to 21 schemata, each obtained from the detailed analysis of many human textual descriptions of the appropriate type.

To avoid this problem we need to consider more seriously *why* texts have different content and structure in different situations. Once we have the reasons for these different choices we can create texts which are appropriate for a new situation without having to analyze human texts generated in that situation. If we can say which features of the situation affect which choices in a text, and why, then we can generate appropriate texts given a whole set of features of the discourse situation. This is the proper domain of text planning and one that is still relatively poorly understood. Although different authors have considered different aspects of the discourse situation (e.g., user's goals [McK88], attitudes [Hov90], and knowledge [Par88]), there is no comprehensive theory of text structure which shows how different choices in text planning depend on different aspects of the situation. Only limited features of the discourse situation have been considered in each system, and the rationale behind the choices made in the text has not always been made fully explicit.

If we can reason about how people change their beliefs, goals, and preferences given some sequence of utterance, we may have the basis for such rational decisions in text planning. It may then be possible to generate an appropriate sequence of utterances given some communicative goal, or desired mental state, and knowledge of the hearer's current mental state. Appelt was able to do this for very short texts [App85], but for longer texts things become more complex. We cannot ignore the conventions governing a text (both those specific to the text type, and general coherence constraints), so we cannot reason solely in terms of the communicative effects of utterances. Also, for many types of text the communicative goal may be ill defined, or at least not fully specified prior to the construction of the text.

One attempt to combine notions of communicative goal with ideas of text coherence is Rhetorical Structure Theory (RST) [MT87a], introduced in the last chapter. Different *rhetorical* (or coherence) relations are associated with the communicative goal that they are used to achieve. For example, the *motivation* relation applies between two text sections where one section motivates an act described in the other. The relation is used when the goal is to increase the reader's desire to do the act. A number of recent text planners have been developed based on this theory, notably [Moo89, MP89] and [Hov88]. However, there are problems with the approach, or at least, with the text planners based on it so far. The different rhetorical relations in the theory relate to a number of different aspects of text structure [Sut89], while the relation between rhetorical relations and rules for rational change in mental state has not been fully described. To generate an appropriate text requires both an explicit representation of the user's knowledge, abilities, and desires in the user model, and the ability to predict the effect of utterances on the user's beliefs etc. Mann and Thomson [MT87b] have proposed such an approach, but it has been only partially realized in implemented systems.

Moore's work (and later work by Maybury [May91b]) at least shows how a text can be planned given some communicative goal, without having to create a new schema for every type of goal. The text plan built up provides a simple representation of the rationale behind a text, and this can be used to provide a context for answering follow-up questions [Moo89]. For example, requests for clarification can take into account what has already been said, the reasons for saying it, and the assumptions made about the user's knowledge in selecting that content.

Moore and Maybury both approach text planning using a simple top down planning approach (also adopted in this work). A top level goal is decomposed into more detailed goals until finally primitive *inform* speech actions are reached. The way goals are decomposed may depend on the user's knowledge and other aspects of the discourse situation, but there are no other major processes involved in the selection and structuring of the text. This approach contrasts somewhat with earlier work, such as [Hov88] and [McK85] where the content of the text was mainly decided beforehand. We would argue that a natural function of the planning process is to determine what to say, as well as how to structure it, and certainly the two processes cannot be completely separated. However, recent work has challenged this basic architecture as conflating too many aspects of text planning into a single uniform process. More complex multi-stage architectures have been proposed [Sut91, MCM91], though it remains to be seen if these will have significantly improved functionality as a result.

As well as these primarily theoretical developments there has been a lot of recent interest in how text generation systems can be incorporated into practical applications. There has been recent research involving the combination of text and graphics [FM90, WAGR91, May91a], the generation of appropriately formatted text [HA91], and the development of improved methods and interfaces for asking follow-up questions after a textual description [MS90, RML92]. Maybury, for example, shows how text planning rules can be extended to include graphical actions, allowing multimedia explanations to be generated. (The EDGE system uses a similar approach, discussed in chapter 6.) Feiner and McKeown [FM90] and Wahlster et al. [WAGR91] both consider more complex issues concerning the combination of text and graphics, such as how to select which to use given some content to convey, and how the detailed planning of one should influence the planning of the other. Moore [MS90] and Reiter, Mellish, and Levine [RML92] both present menu-based interfaces where follow-up questions can be asked, considering such issues as how to decide what questions to make available, and in Moore's work, how to interpret these questions according to context.

The EDGE system uses many of the ideas described above. We show how an appropriate text may be generated given a communicative goal (e.g., to make clear how some particular object works, or to make clear its structure) and detailed assumptions about the user's prior knowledge. We attempt to base the decisions of what to include in the explanations on rational principles, rather than unexplained schemata. The content of the explanation may include both text and graphics, and follow-up questions are available through menus.

3.3   Planning Informative Explanations

This section will consider in more detail the principles that should govern the generation of extended explanations (rather than the principles common to any text), and discuss the problem of generating appropriately *informative* explanations.

An explanation, as we defined it in chapter 1, is something that makes some piece of knowledge clear to the hearer or reader. The most important criterion that we will consider for explanation generation will therefore be the *informativity* of the explanation. Or to put it another way, the most important aspect of the discourse situation that we must be able to take into account is the user's knowledge. The explanation should make sense, linking in with the hearer's existing knowledge, while not containing superfluous information.

Of course, informativity cannot be considered in isolation. In order to be informative a text must also be sufficiently cohesive and coherent. The hearer should also be able to understand the intentional structure of the explanation, knowing why some particular bit of information is being given (in terms of the overall goal) and thus being motivated to try and make sense of what is being conveyed. And in many domains an explanation may only make sense through the appropriate use of graphical actions such as pointing.

The EDGE system attempts to satisfy these principles in the following ways:

- A simple focus model is used both in selecting appropriate pronouns and in constraining the order of text content.
- The explanation is planned from an overall communicative goal, and appropriate markers and meta-comments are used to make the intentional structure clear.
- Graphical actions are used frequently in the "text."

- The explanation is planned so that it should be understood by the hearer, while not including redundant information. This includes deciding what material to include in the explanation and choosing between different ways of explaining it. This issue is discussed further below.

Numerous authors have proposed simple ways of tailoring an explanation or description given assumptions about the user's knowledge. The simplest approach proposed has been simply to leave out bits of a text or explanation which can be assumed already known [MM81, Wei80]. However, although this eliminates much superfluous information, it does not ensure that the remaining information is understandable. To make sense an explanation should be based on familiar concepts. If the required concepts for explaining a topic in a certain way are not already known then either they must be introduced beforehand, or the topic must be explained in some other manner.

So, generating an understandable explanation must involve, at the least, choosing between alternative ways of explaining something and choosing when additional background material should be provided. These are closely interrelated, both depending on the prerequisite topics which are required for some explanation fragment to make sense. An explanation strategy should be chosen to communicate the necessary concepts both efficiently and effectively given the user's prior knowledge.

Simple techniques have been used in the past for each of these issues. To decide on background material, prerequite relationships may be defined among topics, specifying explicitly what topics must already be understood for others to be successfully explained and understood. This approach has been adopted for example in work on curriculum planning, where a sequence of lessons on different topics is planned for an individual user [Mur89, Les88, PM86]. If there is a goal of explaining some topic, and prerequisite topics are not believed to be understood, then these topics are added to the plan. This is a useful approach but is slightly problematic, as the prerequisite topics don't just depend on the topic itself but on the way it is to be explained.

To decide between alternative explanation strategies more "compiled" approaches have been used. An explanation strategy may have an associated constraint, indicating the class of user the strategy is likely to be effective (and efficient) for. At the simplest, the constraint may simply indicate that this strategy is likely to be good for novices (cf.

[Par88]). Slightly more complex, a constraint might indicate that a particular strategy (e.g., *analogy*) is likely to be good for people who know about the analogous object. These rules implicitly allow strategies to be chosen which are likely to be both understandable and efficient.

One important choice concerning the way something is explained is the level of detail (e.g., for a complex process or justification). The level should be chosen so that each step in the sequence of events or rules is understandable. The steps might consist of already known causal events or rules, or failing this they might consist of events or rules made up of known or understandable concepts. Selecting the right level of detail may be complex. In some cases, detailed events/rules may involve unknown concepts, and a higher level description is to be preferred. Wallis and Shortliffe, for example, effectively left out steps in a justification if they were based on unknown (e.g., medical) concepts [WS85]. In other cases, the detailed events may be already familiar to the user and more understandable than the higher level description. Providing such detail may allow the user to understand in detail *why* some process occurs or justification is valid, based on familiar events or rules.

Having decided on a basic strategy for explaining something it may still be possible to leave out some information that is believed to be already understood. However, determining what information is essential to an explanation and what is optional is a fairly complex issue, and depends on the *role* of the information in the explanation and its implicit *relations* with other pieces of information. The sequence in which information is presented may convey such implicit relations (particularly if discourse markers are used). So, even if two concepts are known, the relationship between them (such as sequence or cause) may not be. If it is that relation which is important, then even if the concepts are already understood they should be included in the explanation (unless the implicit relation is known too). For example, if a sequence of events is presented as an explanation of how something works, then it is the fact that a causal relation can be inferred between the events that is important, not the fact of the individual events themselves. Just because the user understands each event doesn't mean that he will learn nothing from the explanation. Similarly, if a proof is being explained to the user, then just because the user knows each step in the proof doesn't make the explanation redundant. The *role* of a proposition in a text influences whether it should or shouldn't be included if already known by the hearer.

This section has outlined some of the issues which should be addressed when generating understandable explanations. The EDGE system attempts to use simple techniques to address the different issues, but does not claim general, ideal solutions. Content planning rules may have preconditions, allowing background information to be included as needed, and constraints, allowing alternative explanation strategies (including level of detail) to be selected. Subgoals may be essential (because of an implicit but inferrable relation between topics) or may be optional.

3.4 The EDGE Explanatory Text Planner

The following sections will describe the EDGE text planning component, and show how it is used to plan the content of an explanation. The system consists primarily of a set of content planning rules and a simple planner. These two main components are described first. Later sections describe further details of the system, and discuss briefly how the approach may be applied in other domains.

3.4.1 Content Planning Rules and Plan Language:

In the EDGE system a simple plan language is used to represent both content and dialogue planning rules. This section will describe this language, motivating and illustrating it with examples from content planning in the circuit domain (analyzed in chapter 2).

Planning rules have six main components: a *name*, which for content planning describes the type of topic being explained; *arguments*, which will be objects or values in the domain; *constraints*, which provide applicability conditions for selecting between alternative planning rules; *preconditions*, which represent goals which should be satisfied if not already believed true; *subgoals*, which are goals which should all be satisfied; and a *template*, which is an English description of the topic, used in giving meta-comments.

The name and arguments of a content planning rule together represent a particular topic which can be explained. For example, the name and argument `how-it-works (device)` represent the topic of how a particular device works. That device will be an object in the domain, and will be specified in the planning process. Constraints on content planning rules refer to properties of the user model or the domain model. If there is more than one rule which can be used to explain the same topic, constraints are used as the main method of selecting between them. Unlike preconditions, the system never attempts to satisfy an unsatisfied constraint.

Preconditions and subgoals are used to distinguish between subtopics that must be explained, even if already known, and subtopics which should only be introduced if not already understood. The preconditions of a rule will normally refer to prerequisite or background information, which needs to be included (if not already known) if the "main" explanation is to make sense. For example, knowledge of the behavior of a device's components helps the user to make sense of the explanation of how that device works, but need not be explained if the user already understands it.

Subgoals reprensent the crucial subtopics in the main explanation. These subtopics will be included even if believed already understood. As discussed in the last section, it is often the sequence in which information is presented which conveys new conceptual information (ie, important relationships between known concepts), so it is important not just to automatically miss out any topics or concepts which are believed already understood. As an example of this, the subgoals when explaining a *process* will be the individual *causal-events* that make up that process. These may be understood individually, but for the process to be understood the whole sequence should (probably) be presented, so the underlying causal and sequential relationships may be inferred.

Of course, it is quite hard to decide exactly what the prerequisite relationships between topics are, what material is optional, and how the two issues interrelate. The approach used in the EDGE system is simple, and not without problems, some of which will be discussed in chapter 7.

An example planning rule illustrating the use of preconditions and subgoals is given in figure 3.1. This example shows that the prerequisite for understanding how a device works is an understanding of the structure of the device, while essential subtopics involved in the explanation include the *process* (i.e., the sequence of events explaining the device's behavior) and the overall *behavior* of the device. There is an implicit *conclusion* or *summary* relation between the process and behavior descriptions — we are explaining the behavior in terms of a process, or sequence of events.

```
c-plan how-it-works (device)
   preconditions: know-user structure (device)
   subgoals: c-goal process (device)
            c-goal behavior (device)
   template: (''how'' (ref device) ''works'')
```

Figure 3.1
Content Planning Rule for Explaining How a Device Works

If a rule has all its constraints and preconditions satisfied, this should mean that the main subtopics should be understandable by the user. Two rules to explain the same topic, both with constraints on applicability, are illustrated in figure 3.2. The first rule describes a device using an analogy with a related known device, while the second describes it by first identifying it as an instance of a known class. In the latter case the subtopics are represented as preconditions — as there is no obvious inferable relation between the topics they can be omitted if already known by the user.

The templates attached to the rules in the figures are used to refer to the topic being explained. For example, a meta-comment might be given saying that the system is about to explain how a light detector circuit works. These templates are *not* used in generating the main content of the explanation — another set of templates is used for this which associates types of propositions with the English which can be used to express those propositions. These latter templates are described in section 3.4.4. (Both sets of templates could be replaced with a natural language sentence generator if required.)

Subgoals of content planning rules may be of various types. They normally consist of other topics to be explained. These may be basic *c-goals* (or content goals), which should always be explained, or *know-user* goals, which should only be explained if not known already. The other types of subgoal allowed are *iterative* goals, which allow a goal to be repeated for a set of different arguments; *d-goals* (or dialogue goals), which invoke dialogue actions (such as *informing*); and graphical actions, invoked by a lisp *call*. Iterative goals are represented by the form `forall <var> in <listexpr> <subgoal>` where `<listexpr>`

```
c-plan structure (device)
    constraints: device-analogy (device)
                 know-user
                     ('structure (device-analogy device))
    subgoals: c-goal compare-structure
                 (device (device-analogy device))
    template: ''what the'' (ref device) ''is like''

c-plan structure (device)
    constraints: device-type (device)
                 know-user ('structure (device-type device))
    preconditions: know-user identity (device)
                   know-user components (device)
                   know-user function (device)
    template: ''what the'' (ref device) ''is like''
```

Figure 3.2
Content Planning Rules for Describing a Device's Structure

should evaluate to a list of items. A subgoal should be created for each binding of <var> in that list. For example, in the first rule in figure 3.3 a *know-user* goal will be created for explaining the behavior of each component of the given device (if not already known).

The only variables in the EDGE planning rules are those specified as arguments to the planning rule. These are bound when the rule is invoked, and used when evaluating the arguments of any subgoals in the rule. For example, if the planning rule argument **device** is bound to **light-unit** then the subgoal **c-goal compare-structure (device (device-analogy device))** would be evaluated to the instantiated goal **c-goal compare-structure (light-unit heat-unit)** (as the specified analogous device to a light detector unit is a heat detector unit). If the goal is an iterative one then it is the list expression that is evaluated, so the goal **forall component in (device-components device) (c-goal behavior (component))** might first be evaluated to give **forall component in (LDR resistor) (c-goal behavior (component))**.

This approach to variable binding contrasts with many text planning systems where general purpose pattern matching is used, allowing variables to be bound in the constraints and subgoals of the planning

```
c-plan components (device)
    preconditions: know-user constituency (device)
                   forall component in
                         (device-components device)
                         (know-user behavior (component))
    template: (''what'' (possref device) ''components do'')

c-plan identity (device)
    subgoals: d-goal inform ((list 'kind-of device
                                   (device-type device)))
    template: (''what kind of device'' (ref device) ''is'')
```

Figure 3.3
Content Planning Rules for Describe a Device's Components and Class

rule, as patterns are matched against the knowledge base or user model
[Moo89, May91b]. The EDGE approach is more efficient though less
powerful, and leads to a slightly less elegant formalization of the rules.
(It was developed partly in order to have an adequately fast system for
evaluation with users, on fairly slow machines.) Another difference compared with planners such as Moore's and Maybury's is that the *effects*
of the plan are not explicitly represented. We just describe what topic
is being explained, and it is up to the user modeling component to determine whether it has in fact been understood. The desired effect of,
say, the rule in figure 3.1 is that the user should understand how the
specified device works.

Approximately 25 content planning rules have been defined in the
EDGE system, with a working subset given in appendix B.1. The set of
rules is based on the content grammar abstracted from the analysis of
human explanations, described in chapter 2, and is specific to the *how
things work* domain. The range of explanations which can be generated
from the planning rules (given different assumptions about the user etc.)
should correspond fairly closely to the range of explanations observed in
the human explanations, partly captured in the content grammar. Note
that the details of these rules and the exact treatment of preconditions
have undergone some evolution over time so the precise form will differ
slightly from earlier publications (e.g. [Caw92, Caw91].).

3.4.2   Planning Algorithm

In planning a potentially interactive explanation it is important not to
commit to the details of the future explanation before one has to. As
assumptions about the user and the current focus in the discourse may
both change in the process of the explanation, detailed future planning
is likely to become redundant. If an explanation was planned out fully
it would probably have to be partly replanned if the system changed
its assumptions about the user's knowledge, for example. Although this
chapter is not immediately concerned with interactive explanations we
will still be concerned to develop the explanation plan in a way that
does not commit to details before this is necessary.

In order to achieve this flexibility the future plan at any instant is
represented as a partially ordered agenda of high level goals still to be
satisfied. Planning proceeds incrementally, so as soon as some primitive
action is planned, it is executed. Planning basically involves the depth-
first hierarchical expansion of goals into subgoals, using the planning
rules to determine the appropriate subgoals. The rest of this section
describes the planning process in more detail.

Initially the system is given a topic to be explained in the form of a
c-goal, such as the following:

```
c-goal how-it-works (light-unit)
```

This goal is placed on the agenda, which represents the remaining
topics to be explained in the explanation. Initially this agenda will only
include a single goal corresponding to the main topic to be explained.

Planning proceeds by selecting a goal from that agenda, and either
executing that "goal" if it corresponds to a primitive action (such as a
graphical action or speech act), or selecting a planning rule which can be
used to satisfy that goal. If a planning rule is selected this will result in
new subgoals being placed on the agenda. These goals will be partially
ordered, based on the following principles:

• Prerequisite goals must be satisfied before subgoals. This is because
they correspond to background information which may be necessary for
the main body of the explanation to make sense.

• Prerequisite goals may be satisfied in any order (though a default is
given) as the topics should be independent of each other. For exam-

ple, when describing a number of different components it is not that important what order they are described in.

• Subgoals should be satisfied in the order given, as there is normally a conceptual relation linking the goals (or rather the topics that the goals are concerned with) which depends on the order. For example, if a causal sequence of events is presented this must be given in the right (causal) order.

• Low level goals should be satisfied before high level goals. This basically enforces depth-first processing where the future plan is not developed any more than it needs to be before execution begins. For example, if the goals on the agenda include one to describe the behavior of a particular component and one to describe the overall *process* explaining the main device's behavior, then the system develops the plan to explain the component behavior, leaving the process description as an unexpanded high level goal.

Ordering information is represented on the agenda by assigning a simple numeric priority value to the goals. The goal which will be taken off the agenda next will be one of those with the lowest value.

Prerequisite topics are initially put on the agenda even if believed understood by the user. (The goal type know-user effectively marks them as prerequisite.)[3] Placing prerequisite topics on the agenda is an attempt to avoid committing to planning decisions before necessary. Assumptions about the user's knowledge could change, so we don't want the system to commit to leaving out some background information until necessary. If assumptions about the user still indicate that the topic is understood when the goal is taken *off* the agenda, then that goal will be discarded.

As mentioned above, the planning process is incremental, using simple depth-first expansion of goals into subgoals. As soon as an executable action is planned it is executed. This means that the future "plan" at any point consists simply of a set of fairly high level topics still to be explained (but not details of how they will be explained). Those topics which are just about to be explained will be given in detail, whereas topics further into the future are only given in outline. Simple incremental hierarchical expansion planning such as this has also been used

---

[3]In fact, the **know-user** goal type currently makes the **preconditions** field of the planning rules largely redundant, though it is retained for clarity.

in Moore's and Maybury's text planners [Moo89, May91b]. For generating non-interactive text the approach is adequate, but there may be arguments for non-incremental approaches (discussed in chapter 7). For interactive explanations the approach has a positive advantage, as changes in assumptions about the user derived through interactions with the user will influence the details of the developing plan without any complex replanning process.

The basic planning algorithm is summarized below:

- A goal is selected from the agenda. The possible goals are determined by the partial order of the agenda. From these the actual selected goal depends first on a simple focus rule[4] and then on the default order of the goals.
- Depending on its type then:

  – If it is a primitive (graphical or linguistic) action it is immediately executed.

  – If it is an iterative call then a goal is put on the agenda for each binding of the iteration variable to the items in the binding list. For example, the goal:

  `forall comp in (LDR resistor) (c-goal behavior (comp))`
  would result in the two new goals:

  `c-goal behavior (LDR)` and

  `c-goal behavior (resistor)`

  – If it is a *know-user* goal AND the associated topic is believed not understood then it is replaced by a *c-goal* for the same topic. Otherwise it is removed from the agenda.

  – If it is a *c-goal* then the set of planning rules is found which can be used to satisfy that goal and which have their constraints satisfied. One of these is selected (currently the first — the default ordering of the rules reflects a simple preference order based primarily on the specificity of the rule). The arguments of the planning rule are bound to the appropriate values in the goal, and used when evaluating the arguments of subgoals and prerequisite goals (including expressions in iterative goals). These

---

[4]The focus rule currently used is very simple. The system compares the objects in focus in the last utterance with the objects mentioned in the goal and prefers goals where there are some objects in common. The representation of focus is discussed again in section 3.4.4 and 4.4.3. More complex rules for focus movement such as used by McKeown [McK85] or suggested by McCoy and Cheng [MC91] could be considered in future work.

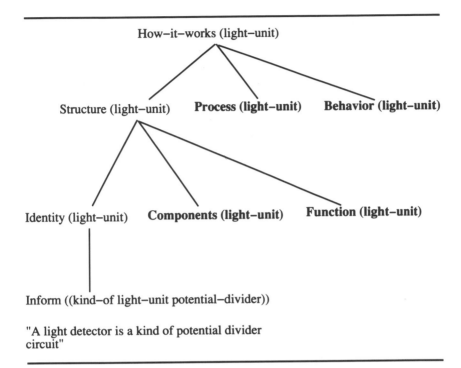

Figure 3.4
Example Partially Completed Discourse Content Plan

instantiated goals are then placed on the agenda.

As planning proceeds a discourse plan (or model) is built up which gives a detailed representation of the past discourse and an outline of the future discourse. When generating interactive explanations this discourse plan will represent both the content being explained and the dialogue with the user. However, in this chapter we are concerned with the planning and representation of the content of the explanation. A simplified example of a partially completed discourse content plan is given in figure 3.4. In this example goals in bold will still be on the agenda, and not yet fully planned or executed. The extension of the discourse model to include dialogue actions, and its use in planning an interactive explanation, will be discussed in chapter 4.

3.4.3   Example Content Planning

Using the set of content planning rules and the simple planner described
above, the system can decide on the content of an explanation given a
topic to explain and assumptions about the user's knowledge. In this
section we will go through a simple example illustrating this basic process
in the *how things work* domain. In particular, we will show how the
planning of the content of the first few utterances of the dialogue in
chapter 1 begins.

For the purpose of this example we will assume that the planning rules
to be used are those given in figures 3.1–3.3. These are a simplified and
restricted set from those used in the actual EDGE system which are
developed further in chapter 6, with a working subset listed in appendix
B.1.

Initially the system is given a topic to explain, and a content goal is
placed on the agenda. In this case we want the system to explain how a
"light detector unit" works, so the following goal is placed on the agenda
and the planning process invoked:

```
c-goal how-it-works (light-unit)
```

The system takes the above goal off the agenda and looks for the set
of planning rules which can be used to satisfy it. The only rule given is
the one in figure 3.1, so this rule is selected, with the argument `device`
bound to `light-unit`. Now the system places the preconditions and
subgoals of the rule on the agenda with appropriately bound arguments,
resulting in the following agenda:

```
know-user structure (light-unit)
c-goal process (light-unit)
c-goal behavior (light-unit)
```

The ordering constraints restrict the prerequisite goal (denoted by the
know-user goal type) to occur before the associated subgoals, and the
subgoals to occur in the order given in the rule. The goals in the above
agenda therefore have a fixed order. The next goal to be taken off the
agenda is the goal that the structure of the light-unit be known.

Now, if the structure were already believed known then the system
would throw out this goal and proceed with explaining the *process*. However, in this case the structure is not already (fully) understood, and so

should be explained. There are two possible rules available for explaining the structure, both given in figure 3.2. The first uses an analogy with a related device, while the second explains the structure by first identifying the device as an instance of a more general circuit type, then describing the components of the circuit, and then its function. The latter rule has its subgoals treated as preconditions — that is, they should only be explained if not already understood. There is a constraint on the first rule that says that the user should already be familiar with the analogous device, while for the second rule the constraint is that the user should be familiar with the more general circuit type. If we assume that only the second constraint holds then new goals will be placed on the agenda as follows:

```
know-user identity (light-unit)
know-user components (light-unit)
know-user function (light-unit)
c-goal process (light-unit)
c-goal behavior (light-unit)
```

Now, in our model the first three goals could potentially be explained in any order (though it would arguably be at least odd to describe the components before identifying the device). However, as the only criterion which can overcome the default order is focus, and each goal has the same focus (the light unit), the default order will hold, and the next item taken off the agenda will be know-user identity (light-unit). If we again assume that the identity of the light-unit (in terms of a more general class of circuits) is not already believed known by the user, then rule 2 in figure 3.3 will be selected to explain this. This rule has a single subgoal which is a discourse goal (denoted *d-goal*) for informing the user of the proposition that one device is an instance of its more general device class. (The version of this rule for interactive discourse has a goal to have an exchange with the user here, but we will consider a simple informing goal for simplicity.)

Anyway, the following goal will be placed on the agenda:

```
d-goal inform ((kind-of light-unit potential-divider)
```

The inform action causes the associated proposition to be presented in natural language, using simple template-based techniques (discussed in the next section). This results in the first utterance:

"A light detector unit is a kind of potential divider circuit."

At this point in the planning process the discourse plan is as represented earlier in figure 3.4. Planning will continue in a similar manner until there are no longer any goals on the agenda, which means that the complete explanation has been generated. An example text generated using this approach, without any dialogue planning, is given in figure 3.5. As it stands the example is slightly incoherent, because of the lack of discourse markers, meta-comments, and links with the diagram. These will be discussed further below, and in chapter 6, where full worked examples of interactive explanations will be given. The examples in chapter 6 include an explanation of a relatively complex circuit, made up of a number of simpler circuits such as the one above. The level of detail at which the *process* description is given in such cases will depend on the assumptions about the user's knowledge, so that each step will be based on known concepts.

3.4.4   Extending the Basic Approach

So far we have seen how simple text planning rules may be used to plan some text content given a topic to explain and assumptions about the user's prior knowledge. However, it is not enough to simply output a list of propositions. The output explanation should obviously be in natural language (e.g., English), making appropriate use of pronouns, discourse markers, and meta-comments (making the structure and function of the text clear), and incorporating graphical actions where appropriate. This section will consider how this is done in the EDGE system. Simple techniques are used, but ones which have proved effective for a practical system.

Generating Natural Language   The EDGE system does not make use of a natural language sentence generator, though this could be incorporated fairly straightforwardly into the basic architecture. Instead we associate with each type of proposition a simple template, with gaps for the objects which will be "arguments" of that proposition. A simple example is the following:

```
proposition: (kind-of device1 device2)
template: ((ref device1) "is a kind of" (name device2))
```

1. A light detector unit is a kind of potential divider circuit.
2. It has the following components:
3. – A fixed resistor.
4. – A light dependent resistor.
5. This component here is a light dependent resistor.
6. When it has a high input light intensity its output resistance is quite low.
7. When it has a low input light intensity its output resistance is quite high.
8. The light detector unit's function is to produce an output voltage that depends on the input light intensity.
9. Suppose its input light intensity is high.
10. When the light dependent resistor has a high input light intensity its output resistance is quite low.
11. The fixed resistor always has a medium output resistance.
12. When the potential divider circuit has a quite low input resistance and a medium input resistance then its output voltage is quite high.
13. Suppose the light detector's input light intensity is low.
14. When the light dependent resistor has a low input light intensity its output resistance is quite high.
15. The fixed resistor always has a medium output resistance.
16. When the potential divider circuit has a quite low input resistance and medium input resistance then its output voltage is quite low.
17. When the light detector unit has a high input light intensity its output voltage is quite high.
18. When it has a low input light intensity its output voltage is quite low.

Figure 3.5
Example Uninterrupted Text

Ref and name are functions that are called when the template is "eval-uated" with its arguments instantiated. The function name returns the English name of some object, while the ref returns either the name or the appropriate pronoun depending on the discourse focus. (An-other function which is defined is possref which obtains the posses-sive pronoun or name.) Given the proposition (kind-of light-unit potential-divider) the template would be used to obtain either the sentence "The light detector unit is a kind of potential divider circuit" or the sentence "It is a kind of potential divider circuit."

Deciding on pronoun use is a complex research topic (see [Sid83, Dal88] for example), and one that we do not address fully here. However, fairly simple methods can be used to give acceptable results. Deciding on whether to use a pronoun requires knowledge of what objects are in *focus* in the preceding discourse. Objects in focus are candidates for pronominalization. So central to our model of pronominalization is a simple focus model.

The EDGE system bases the focus model on the arguments to the goals and subgoals in the discourse plan. For content goals these will be objects and values in the domain model, mentioned in the discourse. Based on the discourse plan there is effectively a stack of focus spaces analogous to Grosz and Sidner's [GS86]. High level goals will have at-tached focus spaces referring to the main objects in focus for a long discourse segment, while low level goals have focus spaces referring to the specific objects in some short subsection of discourse. When we con-sider dialogue plans in the next section we will see that by using goal arguments as a simple model of focus we can also include the main topics being explained (e.g., how the light detector works) as part of the focus model, and so will be able to refer to these using pronouns.

Based on this simple focus model, the rule used to determine when to use a pronoun is the following. If the object was in the focus space of the preceding utterance (i.e., the arguments of the goal which resulted in this utterance include that object) AND the two utterances are both within a higher level discourse segment which has that object in its focus space, then a pronoun is used. This is a fairly conservative algorithm, only allowing pronoun reference to the preceding sentence, and not allowing references to the preceding sentence where that sentence is part of a different discourse segment with a different focus (i.e., where there is an "accidental" connection between the objects in adjacent utterances).

However, although the resulting text may occasionally be more verbose than needed, the referents of the pronouns should be easily identified.

Incorporating Graphical Actions Another extension to the basic approach is to allow graphical actions to be incorporated into the explanation. This is especially important in the *how things work* domain. As we saw in section 3.2, this is a very active area of current research. There are difficult issues concerning how to decide between conveying things graphically and textually, and how the planning of graphics should interact with the planning of text. The EDGE system uses simple techniques somewhat similar to those developed later by Maybury (1991). Graphical actions are simply incorporated as part of a text planning rule; so given a goal such as to get the user to be able to identify an object in a diagram, the planning rule will have subgoals to point at the diagram and inform the user of the name of the device. This approach will be discussed further in chapter 6.

Adding Discourse Markers and Meta-Comments If the user is to understand the function and structure of the discourse then discourse markers and meta-comments should be added where appropriate. Previous work on text generation has focused on the markers that are used between two sections of text linked by a particular rhetorical relation (e.g., [Moo89, Hov88]. While acknowledging the importance of this work, the EDGE system concentrates on the meta-comments and discourse markers that are used to indicate a new topic in the discourse.

While utterances conveying normal propositional content refer to the domain objects being conveyed, topic opening meta-comments refer to topics which are about to be explained. These topics are represented in content goals. Meta-comments and markers are therefore introduced through a second level of planning rules which take content goals (and hence topics) as their arguments. These rules are based on the models of discourse discussed in chapter 2, section 2.2.1 [SC75], with rules for describing the structure of different kinds of *transactions* on a topic, *exchanges* between the participants, and dialogue *moves*. The rules are developed further in the next chapter as they are extended to form the basis of the EDGE dialogue planner.

Figure 3.6 illustrates two of the dialogue planning rules which are used when planning opening and closing sequences around topics. The rules can be used for non-interactive discourse to plan markers and meta-

```
d-plan informing.transaction (content-goal)
   subgoals: d-goal boundary.exchange (content-goal 'open)
             d-goal teaching.exchanges (content-goal)
             d-goal boundary.exchange (content-goal 'close)

d-plan boundary.exchange (content-goal type)
   constraints: equal (type 'open)
   subgoals: d-goal framing.move (type)
             d-goal focusing.move (content-goal type)
```

Figure 3.6
Rules for Planning Opening and Closing Sequences

comments to introduce a topic — this will be the opening boundary
exchange. The first rule simply says that a transaction on a topic consists
of an opening exchange, a sequence of teaching exchanges, and a closing
exchange. The second rule says that an opening exchange for tutorial
discourse consists of a *framing* move and a *focusing* move. These framing
and focusing moves correspond to a topic opening discourse marker and
meta-comment(s) on what is about to be explained.

Given some topic to be explained, an *informing transaction* goal is
placed on the agenda, with the topic as its argument. For example:

```
informing.transaction ((how-it-works (light-unit)))
```

The normal planning process described above will cause this goal to
be expanded into the following:

```
boundary.exchange ((how-it-works (light-unit)) open)
teaching.exchanges ((how-it-works (light-unit)))
boundary.exchange ((how-it-works (light-unit)) close)
```

Now, an opening boundary exchange will be expanded into a framing
move and a focusing move, which in turn are realized as a discourse
marker such as "OK" or "Right" and meta-comment(s) on the topic. In
this case this will result in the opening utterance:

"Right, I'm going to explain how the light detector unit works."

Extra meta-comments may be added (as part of the focusing move) which refer to the difficulty or importance of the topic (cf. [ZP86]). For example, if the difficulty level of the topic is greater than the level of expertise of the user (see chapter 5) the following may be added:

"It is quite complicated."

Note that the pronoun *it* is used here to refer to the topic, *how the light detector works*, as the topic is itself now included in our model of focus.

The *teaching exchanges* rule causes control to pass back to the content planning rules by placing a content goal on the agenda based on the topic to be explained, i.e.:

```
c-goal how-it-works (light-unit)
```

Content planning then proceeds as described earlier, so the next utterance (given the same assumptions about the user's knowledge as before) will be:

"A light detector unit is a kind of potential divider circuit."

The approach presented so far allows opening and closing statements to be generated for the main topic being explained. However, some of the major subtopics in a complex explanation should also have markers and meta-comments indicating what is to follow. There is a slight problem here. Whether or not a meta-comment is used should depend on the complexity of what is about to follow, yet using our simple planning approach based on top down expansion of goals into subgoals this is hard to determine. The EDGE system avoids this issue by allowing *subtransaction* subgoals in the content planning rules. These subgoals occur if a subtopic is likely to be a major one, and hence needs opening markers and (possibly) meta-comments. The goals may have an extra argument indicating the functional role of the associated content goal, allowing markers to be added depending on implicit rhetorical relations. Two such goals are illustrated in the full version of the how-it-works rule, given in figure 3.7. The role value *open* simply indicates that the goal represents a new topic to be marked with a "topic opening" dis-

```
c-plan how-it-works (device)
   preconditions: know-user structure (device)
   subgoals: d-goal sub.transaction
                      ((c-goal process (device)) 'open)
             d-goal sub.transaction
                      ((c-goal behavior (device)) 'summary)
   template: (''how'' (ref device) ''works'')
```

Figure 3.7
Content Planning Rule for Explaining How a Device Works: Full Version

course marker, while *summary* indicates that the goal has a summary
relationship with the preceding one, and should be marked as such.

There are problems with this approach. First, it is hard to say defini-
tively in the content rules whether a subtopic will be of sufficient complexity to require an introductory marker or meta-comment, as the
complexity of a part of an explanation will depend both on the particular object being explained and on the user's knowledge. Second,
marking functional roles in this way is a less elegant solution than approaches such as Moore's and Hovy's based on rhetorical structure theory [Moo89, Hov88]. These issues will be discussed further in chapter 7.

Applying Approach to Other Domains So far all the examples
given have been concerned with how simple electronic circuits work.
Further details of this domain (such as the underlying device models
used) will be given in chapter 6. However, the same basic approach may
be applicable in many other domains and types of explanation where
there is some fairly complex topic to be conveyed. It should be possible
to define the topic in terms of subtopics and prerequisite topics and write
content planning rules on the basis of these relations.

We will therefore consider how we might go about generating explanations in two other domains. First, we may want to explain how to do
some complex task, such as mending a device or cooking a meal. There
are definite subtopics corresponding to the subtasks [Gro77], and prerequisite topics which correspond to the concepts which must be familiar for
the subtask descriptions to make sense. The level of detail at which the
tasks are presented should depend on the expertise of the user, so that

```
c-plan how-to (task)
    preconditions: forall object in (task-objects task)
                        (know-user identity (object))
    constraints: know-user how-to (task)
    subgoals: inform (do-user (task))

c-plan how-to (task)
    preconditions: forall object in (task-objects task)
                        (know-user identity (object))
    subgoals: forall subtask in (task-subtasks task)
                  (c-goal how-to (subtask))
```

"This device here is an electric mixer.
Mix up the ingredients using the electric mixer.
Roll out the cookies.
Put them in the oven."

Figure 3.8
Simple Planning Rules for Explaining Tasks

explanations are always given in terms of subtasks which the user knows how to execute.

Second, we may want to present a story or narrative that depends on the user's knowledge of the background setting. The setting of the story may be viewed as prerequisite information, while the events may be viewed as part of the main subtopic.

In the task domain, the task description follows closely the structure of the task, represented in the domain model. The content planning rules can therefore be very simple. Figure 3.8 presents two rules which allow objects to be described if not already known (e.g., "This device here is an electric mixer") and allows the level of detail at which tasks are described to depend on the user's knowledge (e.g., just saying "Mix up the ingredients" rather than explaining how in detail). This is obviously an oversimplification of the process of describing tasks effectively but provides a simple example of content planning in another domain.

Figure 3.9 presents two simple rules for generating a narrative. Narratives are discussed in more detail in [May91b, ch. 5] for example, and in older work on story generation such as [Mee76]. The rules in

```
c-plan narrative (story)
   preconditions: know-user setting (story)
   subgoals: forall episode in (story-episodes story)
             (c-goal episode (episode))

c-plan setting (story)
   preconditions: forall person in (story-characters story)
                   (know-user character (person))
                  know-user location ((story-location story))
```

"Once upon a time there was a haunted house in the middle of nowhere. One day Jim and Fred set out to explore the haunted house."

Figure 3.9
Simple Planning Rules for Stories

the figure are based on Rumelhart's story grammar rules [Rum75], but adapted so that the narrative will depend on the user's prior knowledge. In this example, if we are giving a narrative about two children, Fred and Jim, and a haunted house, then the story could begin either with "Once upon a time there was a haunted house in the middle of nowhere" or with "Once upon a time there were two children called Fred and Jim" depending on whether the user had already been told about Fred and Jim, or about the haunted house.

For both tasks and stories it may be appropriate to begin with a discourse marker and/or meta-comment indicating what you are about to explain. This can be done using exactly the same dialogue planning rules as discussed in section 3.4.4, allowing opening statements such as:

"OK, I'm going to tell you the story of Jim and Fred in the haunted house."

or

"Right, I'm going to explain to you how to make cookies."

By using the full set of dialogue planning rules, interactive task descriptions and stories can be presented where the user has the chance to ask about characters and events in stories or subtasks or objects in task descriptions. However, as this research has only very briefly explored how these other types of explanation should be represented, we will not discuss this in more detail but leave it as an interesting area for further work.

3.5 Conclusion

This chapter has focused on how extended explanatory text may be planned given a topic to explain and assumptions about the user's prior knowledge. While acknowledging the range of principles governing text structure (and the ongoing research which addresses the different principles) the EDGE system has focused on the *informativity* of the text. However, we have also considered how the *intentional structure* of the text may be made explicit through meta-comments, and how to include graphical actions.

One major limitation of the EDGE system is the relative domain specificity of the content planning rules, and the (related) limited treatment of discourse coherence. Improvements might result from making more of the rhetorical structure explicit (combining ideas from [Moo89], [May91b], and this work). Another possible problem concerns the simple planning architecture used (cf. [MCM91, Sut91]). Uniform top down planning may prove an inadequate general framework for text planning.

Some of these problems and limitations will be discussed further in chapter 7. However, for our purposes the approach seems simple and effective and allows interactive explanations to be generated where the details of the explanation will be influenced by the changing assumptions about the user. The managing of the dialogue in such interactive explanations will be the subject of the next chapter.

4 Managing the Dialogue with the User

In the last chapter the content planning part of the EDGE discourse generator was described. However, to extend this to deal with interactive explanations we need to consider how interactions with the user can be managed within a complex explanation, and how they should influence the way that explanation develops.

In the first two sections we will discuss in general terms some of the principles which govern the organization of dialogue, and how they have influenced the development of dialogue systems. This will be followed by a discussion of the particular problem of managing an interactive explanation, and a detailed description of the EDGE dialogue planner.

4.1 Explaining the Organization of Dialogues

In chapter 2 we saw how discourse grammars have been developed which illustrate the normative structure of particular types of discourse, such as tutorial discourse. We began to show how such a grammar could be extended to capture the organization of explanatory dialogues. However, when discussing the limitations of the model we suggested that it failed to provide an explanatory model. An explanatory model should account for *why* people say what they do, when they do. If we have such a model a system may better be able to generate utterances appropriate to the situation.

In this section we will discuss and contrast two very different areas of research that have something to say about how conversation really works, as opposed to how it is organized. The first comes from research in artificial intelligence (AI) (and certain areas of philosophy), where language is viewed as purposeful action, planned to achieve changes in the hearer's mental states, and through that to achieve desired changes in the world. The second area, conversation analysis, is a subfield of sociology. Work on conversation analysis is concerned more with how the conventional organization of conversation enables the participants to make local, collaborative decisions about how it develops, and to repair any problems with the interaction. Models of language based on plans and mental states are largely rejected, in favor of *situated action* where each utterance is constructed and interpreted according to the immediate, local context. Although this latter work does not always immediately lend itself to computational modeling, conversation analysts have provided detailed studies of particular dialogue phenomena which are increasingly being considered by those working on computational models of dialogue.

4.1.1 Intention-Based Models of Language

Intention-based models of language have been developed within artificial intelligence from their roots in philosophy [Aus75]. Language is seen as purposeful behavior, and making sense of language involves the recognition of that purpose. Early work focused on trying to recognize the goals behind individual utterances, and using that recognized goal to make more helpful responses to questions (e.g., [AP80]). However, more recent work has been concerned with modeling extended dialogue where each participant may have goals and plans. Some of the basic theoretical ideas are given in [CMP90], and their application to dialogue systems is briefly mentioned in section 4.2.

A clear illustration of the basic ideas can be taken from work by Power in the 1970s [Pow79]. He showed how extended dialogues could result directly from the domain goals of the participants. He did this by developing a system where two computer "robots" (computer agents) cooperated through dialogue in order to achieve a simple task in a simple artificial world. Power's world consisted of a door and a bolt, with the robots initially at either side of the door. Each robot had various capabilities, such as being able to see or to push the bolt, and various beliefs, such as believing that pushing the door opens it. Their capabilities and knowledge were distributed so that tasks could only be achieved jointly, through collaboration. A robot might begin with a goal, such as to open the door, and have to cooperate with the other robot in order to do this. The dialogue would result directly from this goal-driven behavior.

A simple planner could be used by each robot to reason about how to achieve its goal. When the plan involved something which the robot did not know or could not do, but which the other robot might know or do, then an exchange would be initiated. These exchanges might involve getting attention, making something known, finding something out, or getting something done. A *conversational procedure* was defined for each type of exchange, specifying the respective actions of the two participants. A robot would plan to achieve its goal until it met an obstacle which it believed the other could help with, then a conversational procedure would be chosen and initiated. The other robot would recognize the procedure and be constrained to take the appropriate actions (though it could interrupt to check on the state of the world or to comment on the other's plan). Following an exchange, the world view of each robot would be updated, and then the planning would continue where it left off. This would result in an extensive dialogue, illustrated by the extract below:

John: 1. Mary.
Mary: 2. Yes.
John: 3. I want to suggest a goal.
Mary: 4. Go ahead.
John: 5. Will you help me get in?
Mary: 6. By all means.
John: 7. Shall we make a plan?
        [...]

Mary: 22. John.
John: 23. Yes.
Mary: 24. May I ask you something?
John: 25. Go ahead.
Mary: 26. Is the door open?
John: 27. No.
Mary: 28. I suggest that we get the door open and then you move.
        [...]

Power's dialogues tend to be fairly long-winded, partly because his "robots" have no real notion of shared plans, and their cooperative behavior is limited to responding directly to questions. This type of model has been developed somewhat in [HI85, Car92]. However, the approach clearly demonstrates how a dialogue involving different types of exchanges can result directly from a single domain goal.

4.1.2   Conversation Analysis

A contrasting view of how dialogue "works" can be seen in work on *conversation analysis*. Conversation analysis is primarily concerned with the workings of everyday conversation, which may have no obvious purpose or direction.[1] In order to understand this, conversations are transcribed and analyzed in minute detail, with every slight gesture or pause

---

[1]Hobbs and Evans, however, show how even everyday conversation can be partially explained in terms of planned behavior, given *social* goals such as to create a particular impression [HE79].

viewed as potentially significant in the workings of the interaction. Analysts seek to discover what sense each participant makes of the other's (or others') utterances by using later utterances as a resource, revealing something of this understanding. In general they avoid explaining language behavior in terms of rules, plans, and mental states, but instead look at how the shared conventions (or methods) of everyday conversation help enable robust communication and the local, situated, collaborative development of the conversation [Suc87].

Conversation analysis represents a contrasting approach for analyzing and viewing language. However, it also provides us with a "candy store" of insights about the way people use language in everyday conversation. There have been studies, for example, of the way people open and close conversations, how they recover from misunderstandings, and how they manage to smoothly shift from one participant speaking to another. Some of the results can be formalized in terms of conversational "rules," providing preferences and expectations concerning what will follow. However, analysts are quick to emphasise that these rules should not be viewed as prescriptive in any way. Conversation analysis (and its parent discipline of ethnomethodology) is concerned with the way people use these rules, as much as with the rules themselves.

It is unclear how far work from conversation analysis can be applied to the design of human-computer dialogue systems. It places much emphasis on the minutiae of face-to-face interaction, and normally avoids rigid formalization. However, there are a number of directly applicable and useful insights, summarized below:

Turn Taking One of the early concerns of conversation analysts was how people manage turns at conversation. Turns are managed so that control passes between participants with virtually no detectable pause between utterances. Sacks, Schegloff, and Jefferson (who dominated early work in the field) suggested that there were predictable *Transition Relevance Points* (TRPs) in conversation, where control could switch to another party. These might be after a word, phrase, or sentence, but could be predicted in advance by the other party [SSJ78]. At such points, a simple rule system would determine who would be expected to talk next. If the speaker explicitly selected another person, that person would be expected to speak next. Otherwise, anyone could come in. If no other person contributed, the first speaker would continue. Note that these rules emphasize the interactive nature of even continuous talk. There may still be TRPs where another speaker could potentially contribute, and even the absence of comment represents a contribution to the dialogue. This method of turn taking also means that the length of any turn is rarely prescribed in advance, and can be influenced both by the speaker (in selecting TRPs) and the hearer (in choosing whether to take the floor).

Adjacency Pairs   Another feature of local conversational organization is the way utterances provide expectations for subsequent utterances. So, a question will provide an expectation that an answer will follow, and the following utterance (whatever the surface form) will tend to be interpreted as an answer to the question. Such pairs (e.g., question-answer, greeting-greeting) are referred to as *adjacency pairs*. The second part of the pair is *conditionally relevant* on the first. Although this basic insight is a simple one, the way these sequential expectations are used in making sense of conversation is quite subtle, and discussed in more detail in [Lev83, ch. 6] for example.

Repair   One vital aspect of conversation is the way people recover from errors and misunderstandings. Such repairs can be classified in terms of who initiates the repair, who does the repair, and what turn the repair occurs in after the initial problematic utterance. In human conversation there appear to be preferences for *self-repair* [SJS77], though this may be initiated by the other person. Repairs can occur in the third, fourth, or later turn after the problematic utterance [Sch88].

Insertion Sequences and Side Sequences   Utterances in an adjacency pair need not necessarily be contiguous. For example, a question may be followed by a clarification question and answer pair before being replied to. These are referred to as *insertion sequences*. More general types of interruptions are *side sequences*, where a topic is interrupted to be later resumed. These have been discussed by Jefferson [Jef72].

Opening and Closing Sequences   Another feature of conversations is how they are opened and closed. Common sequences of utterances are used, effectively to negotiate the beginning and end of a conversation.

For example, telephone conversations frequently end with a four part sequence such as:

A: OK
B: OK
A: Bye
B: Bye

The *pre-sequence* of "OK"s is used to negotiate the end of the conversation, allowing each participant to "pass over" the opportunity of continuing. The "Bye"s are used in final leave taking and imply a joint decision to close the conversation. These are conventional patterns of conversation which enable local, collaborative decisions about the length of the conversation.

Some of the dialogue phenomena discussed in work on conversation analysis seem to be partially explainable in terms of a belief/intention-based approach. For example, opening and closing exchanges can be partly explained in terms of achieving the mutual belief that some topic or conversation should be begun or ended. However, there are some features of language use which are solely convention-based, such as the convention of giving three items when presenting a list. Others are influenced by a preference for enabling participants to avoid *losing face* to the other participant, or forcing them to lose face. For example, the preference for *self-repair* in conversation may be partly to avoid the speaker losing face by being corrected. Work in conversation analysis provides us with insights about important dialogue phenomena, and indicates where a purely intention-based or naively rule-governed approach may fail. Some of these ideas are discussed in [Suc87, Lev83, Woo90].

Recent work on the workings of conversation strongly influenced by conversation analysis includes that of Fox [Fox87] and that of Clark and Schaefer [CS89]. Fox discusses how participants in a dialogue may *retrospectively reinterpret* utterances based on later contextual information. This is important if the participants are to recover from past misinterpretations, but people can also deliberately cause such reinterpretations, for example, to avoid losing face because of the failure of the original utterance.

Clark and Schaefer discuss how people come to jointly know that an utterance was correctly understood. They call the unit of discourse through which this is achieved a discourse *contribution*, and argue that this unit of discourse is more fundamental to the workings of dialogue than, for example, the exchange. Of course, participants can never be certain about the other's interpretation, but must have evidence "sufficient for the current purposes." Evidence of understanding may include the way the other's next utterance follows on logically, the other's acknowledgments ("OK"s, and "Uhuh"s), or the other reexpressing the meaning of the utterance. Walker has recently looked at how aspects of this model can account for *redundancy* in dialogue, and provides a more formal account of the way types of evidence for understanding are used [Wal92].

4.1.3   Summary: Factors Influencing the Organization of Dialogues

The two areas of research discussed above are very different. Although both view language as purposeful action, the way they see that action developing is rather different. While the former emphasizes the plans of the participants, the latter emphasizes shared conversational resources and flexible situated action. However, the strands of research are not fundamentally incompatible. Conversation analysis certainly does not reject the notion that a dialogue may be influenced by the participants' goals. It just emphasizes that rules and plans cannot be viewed in an overly simplistic manner, as dictating the way a dialogue will progress. At the same time, work on formal plan-based accounts of language is beginning to take more and more account of the collaborative nature of interaction.

Although there is as yet no overarching theory of human interaction which provides a comprehensive model of how dialogue works, different insights can be gathered from the different areas. Each area is concerned with how people make sense of utterances in a dialogue and choose what to say next. The participants' goals are undoubtedly important, though perhaps overemphasized in recent AI models. Conventional rules, some culture-dependent, are also important, and may allow us to use language effectively without an exhaustive analysis of intentions. For example, a greeting may be provided in response to a greeting without analysing the intentions behind that greeting!

There are a number of factors influencing the development of dialogues that have been neglected in the discussion above but are important in the development of dialogue systems. First, a dialogue must be *coherent.* This is an aspect of the local situated nature of conversation — people may decide moment by moment how a conversation may be coherently continued. The coherent options depend in part on the discourse *focus,* as discussed in section 3.1. Roughly speaking, a participant should not suddenly introduce new topics, but should make their utterances connect with what was said before. If apparently unrelated topics are introduced, then expressions such as "Anyway, that reminds me.." should be used to make the transition clear.

Second, dialogues depend on the roles and responsibilities of the participants (discussed in chapter 2). In all dialogues each participant has some responsibility for determining the course of the dialogue and for ensuring that utterances are understood in the intended manner. However, in some types of discourse the roles of the participants mean that the responsibilities are unbalanced. For example, in parent-child or teacher-student interactions the interactions expected and permitted of each participant are quite different. (See [MF91] for a discussion of such asymmetries in dialogue.) It is at least difficult to capture the effects of these different roles and responsibilities in a purely intention-based model.

4.2   The Development of Dialogue Systems

In this section we will briefly discuss how these different perspectives on language use have been used in the development of human-computer dialogue systems. In particular, we will discuss how a system can both provide opportunities for and make sense of user utterances and select appropriate utterances itself.

4.2.1   Dealing with User Input

A dialogue system may accept user input in natural language, or through a menu-based interface. If the user's utterances are in natural language then the system must be able to interpret them in the context of the overall interaction. If a menu-based approach is used then the system must be able to provide appropriate menu options. Either way, the system may use expectations about what the user might say next. In a menu-based system, these expectations may be used in providing appropriate menu options. For example, if the possible user utterances at some point in the discourse include either answering the system's questions or interrupting with a clarification question, then appropriate menu options may be provided for these. In a natural language system the expectations may be used, for example, to work out the possible referents of pronouns or other anaphoric expressions.

These expectations will normally be based on the assumption that the discourse will be coherent and rational. Answers usually follow questions, topics lead on to related topics, and sequences of utterances often have an underlying unifying purpose. This notion of coherence and rationality in discourse may be represented in many ways. The content of the dialogue may be based on the goals of the participants, on *focus* rules which represent how new objects can be coherently introduced [MC91, McK85], and on genre-specific discourse conventions (e.g., for the structure of narratives). However, the structure of the dialogue also consists of opening and closing sequences, repair sequences, and interruptions, for example. These may also be influenced by the participants' goals (as illustrated in Power's work), or represented using conventional rules, based on a discourse grammar or abstracted from ideas in conversation analysis.

The term *discourse model* is often used to refer to the model of the ongoing interaction which provides such expectations, based on assumptions of coherence and rationality.[2] Discourse models may vary widely, some being based primarily on a discourse grammar, some on plans and focus, and some including genre-specific information. Ferrari and Reilly [FR86], Wachtel [Wac86], and Bilange [Bil91] all use a model based on a discourse grammar (similar to Sinclair and Coulthard's [SC75]) to provide contextual interpretations of natural language utterances. The grammar captures expected sequences of types of interaction with the user. Frohlich and Luff [FL90] use rules from conversation analysis to provide a very flexible menu-based interface accommodating repair, openings and closings of topics, etc. Carberry uses a model of the user's plans and goals, inferred by the system [Car89], to interpret ambiguous utterances. Polanyi [Pol87] and Grosz and Sidner [GS86] have devel-

---

[2]Though see [Jon91] for further uses and representations of discourse models.

oped more general theoretical models of discourse structure. Polanyi's model is essentially syntactic, capturing a range of types of conventional discourse relations. Grosz and Sidner's model is based strongly on the intentions of the participants', incorporating focus within the same framework (as briefly discussed in chapter 2). Discourse models such as these, as well as providing expectations about subsequent discourse, may enable the semantic relations and intentions behind a sequence of utterances to be inferred.

A discourse model may also provide different preferences or likelihoods for different types of utterances. For example, in a discussion of some topic the most likely next utterance is a continuation of that topic. Less likely are new topics, or sudden interruptions. If the system has just asked a question the most likely response is an answer. Less likely are clarification questions, or requests for a change of topic. Jullien and Marty, for example, capture these different kinds of expectation using an *expectation stack*, linked to a model of the user's likely *deviations* from the projected course of the dialogue [JM89]. Litman and Allen [LA87] provide for a slightly more limited range of deviations (such as interruptions), using discourse plans to represent how a participant's domain plans may be realized through dialogue.

Any interpretation of user utterances in a natural language dialogue is liable to error. This problem is particularly acute for speech dialogue systems using a telephone connection with the user. The connection may be poor, the system's real-time speech understanding may be imperfect, and elliptical and ambiguous user utterances may be hard to make sense of given limited contextual information. In these situations, as well as using a discourse model to aid in interpretation, ways of *confirming* interpretations (e.g., by reiterating part of the utterance in the reply) and *repairing* misunderstandings are important. The SUNDIAL project (e.g., [Bil91]) has been concerned with incorporating such confirmations and repair in a general speech-based dialogue system.

4.2.2 Selecting System Utterances

Selection of system utterances should be based primarily on the system's goals and plans (though discourse conventions may also be used, automatically following a greeting with a greeting for example). In a cooperative dialogue, where the system's goal is to help the user, the system's goal may be based on the user's. If the user wants to book an airline ticket, then the system's goal will be to obtain and provide the information required for the booking.

In any extended sequence of interactions there may be one participant who dominates and leads the dialogue. When the dominant participant is the user, the system, in order to be cooperative, may need to infer the goals behind the user's sequence of utterances (cf. [Car89, McK88]). When the dominant participant is the system, the system will have to plan a dialogue to achieve its goals, possibly taking account of user initiative within that goal-driven interaction. Jullien and Marty, for example, show how a system's information gathering plan can be revised and extended based on user initiative (where the user deviates from the system's intitial plan) [JM89]. The system will attempt to reorder topics so that they follow the topics introduced by the user, and extend plans to deal with any misunderstandings that emerge.

If the participants have more equal roles then the system must reason about both its own and the user's plan, and consider how shared plans may be established. Theoretical groundwork for this kind of approach is being developed by Grosz and Sidner [GS90] and by Cohen and Levesque [CL91], while a more practical approach is being pursued by Traum, for the TRAINS dialogue system at Rochester [Tra91]. Traum includes representations not only of the system's and user's plans and beliefs, but of the system's and user's *proposed* plans and beliefs (which may or may not have been accepted by the other participant) and the system's and user's *shared* plans, which the system believes have been agreed by both parties. Dialogue actions may result in a plan or belief being moved between these different spaces, so the user accepting a system-proposed plan would result in the plan becoming a shared plan. Traum is also developing an extended classification of different kinds of speech action which can accommodate turn taking, negotiation, and repair within a single framework.

4.2.3   Conclusion

The particular techniques used in the development of a dialogue system depend on the nature of the application. The task may require that the dialogue is dominated by the system, by the user, or neither; take place in natural language, speech, or simply menus; have a well defined goal or an illdefined one. However, whatever the task, some kind of discourse model is required, and some way of selecting system utterances based on the system's overall goal. The discourse model may be based on conventional rules, or on the participants' plans and intentions.

In the long term we need to consider how domain-independent dialogue systems can be developed which take into account both the plans and intentions of the participants and conventional practices. These conventional conversational practices (such as methods of turn taking and conversational closings) are designed to enable local, context-dependent, collaborative decisions. They therefore cannot be ignored. It is unlikely that they will all be reduced to complex intention-based decisions, and even if they could, for current practical systems it is useful to explicitly represent conventional conversational structure.

The EDGE system uses a primarily "convention-based" dialogue grammar (represented as simple planning rules) to manage the interaction with the user. However, the content of the dialogue is based on the system's plan to make known some complex concept. This content plan may be revised based on user initiative (as in [JM89]). The discourse model includes both the organization of the content and the organization of the interactions with the user. The next section will describe in more detail the type of dialogue modeled and the requirements of the dialogue system.

4.3   Generating Explanatory Dialogues

So far we have considered in general terms how people make sense of and select utterances in a dialogue, and how this has influenced the design of dialogue systems. In this section we will focus on explanatory dialogues, starting off by identifying the particular type of explanatory dialogue which we will attempt to model, extending the discussion in chapters 1 and 2. We will go on to present some simple criteria for a model of such dialogues, before discussing in detail the EDGE model of explanatory dialogues.

4.3.1   Types of Explanatory Dialogue

In chapter 2 we saw that the organization of explanatory dialogues varied widely, and appeared to depend on the roles and responsibilities adopted by the participants. We loosely characterized these using terms like *expert-dominant tutorial* and *novice-dominant informing*. In the expert-dominant tutorial dialogues the expert is responsible for making sure the novice learns the explained material, and the expert dominates the interaction. It is the expert who appears to have the goal of making the novice understand the material, with the novice's goal of understanding less apparent. The expert can choose what to explain, as the novice has no apparent independent explanatory need.

In the novice-dominant informing dialogue the novice dominates the interaction, having particular information needs. The responsibility for understanding the material either lies with the novice or is shared. Our example dialogues were initiated by the expert, but the novice rapidly took over driving the interaction, as the expert was not giving the information required. However, more commonly the novice will initiate an explanatory dialogue by asking a question, and drive it by asking further clarification and elaboration questions until their explanatory need is satisfied.

Moore's explanation system is concerned with this latter type of explanatory dialogue [Moo89]. She used a text planner based on rhetorical relations (mentioned in chapter 3) to plan responses to user uestions in an expert system advisory interaction. However, the main emphasis of her work was on how the system could respond to the user's follow-up questions in a context-dependent way. The dialogue wasn't just seen as a sequence of independent questions, but each follow-up question was analyzed in the light of the explanation just generated. This allowed the system to disambiguate ambiguous questions (such as "Why?" and "Huh?") and to plan responses that depended on the prior discourse. Each system response was typically a few utterances long, and the system had no overall plan concerning what to convey in the whole dialogue.

In this work we focus more on explanatory dialogues which are primarily dominated by the expert (i.e., the system). The system has a goal to make the user understand some complex concept, which might take many utterances and many interactions with the user to explain. The user may influence the dialogue through clarification questions, interrupting the main body of the explanation or asked at the end, but may not redirect its entire course. This presents different problems from those considered by Moore, though the approach developed is complementary to hers.

4.3.2   Principles Influencing the EDGE Dialogue Planner

The purpose of the EDGE dialogue planner is to select an appropriate sequence of dialogue actions given an explanatory goal (to convey some complex piece of knowledge) and assumptions about the user's prior knowledge. The system must plan how to convey the information, while checking that the user is following and understanding. At the same time the system should give the user the opportunity to initiate dialogue actions themselves, and be able to respond to such actions. The dialogue generated should be:

Coherent: Obeying conventions governing the organization of dialogue, as well as rules for shift in dialogue focus.

Individualized: With the selection of dialogue actions dependent on assumptions about the user's knowledge, and further on the roles adopted by system and user.

Flexible: Giving the user the opportunity to contribute to the dialogue and influence how it progresses.

Responsive: Responding to changing assumptions about the user's knowledge and to changes in discourse focus, rather than being based on a rigid plan.

Robust: Able to respond appropriately when the dialogue "fails" and the user is confused.

The EDGE system attempts to achieve this using simple planning rules, defining a discourse grammar for explanatory dialogues. This is based primarily on the analyses in chapter 2, but is further influenced by work on conversation analysis. Dialogue planning rules aren't viewed as *determining* the course of the dialogue but as providing *opportunities* for user intervention and repair. The set of dialogue rules also define the range of *coherent* dialogues, with constraints on the rules determining how different dialogue actions may be selected depending on the user's assumed knowledge and the roles of the system and user. The system is responsive to changes in discourse focus and changing assumptions about the user, as the explanatory dialogue is not fully planned out in advance but developed incrementally.

This approach is an effective and computationally tractable way of selecting dialogue actions, especially where the system has the dominant

role. A purely intention-based approach was not chosen as it is harder to
incorporate within such a framework dialogue decisions which are based
primarily on convention, which provide opportunities for user contributions and repair, and which depend on the roles of the participants.

The planning rules developed allow a range of dialogue phenomena,
including: *opening and closing exchanges*, where particular sequences
of conversational moves are used to negotiate the beginnings and ends
of topics and conversations (depending on participant roles); *interruptions*, where a clarification sequence may take place part way through
an explanation, with that explanation resumed appropriately at the end
of the sequence; and *remedial and repair sequences*, where the system
responds to the user's apparent confusion or misunderstanding. The
details of these rules are given below.

4.4   Dialogue Planning in the EDGE System

Planning an explanatory dialogue in the EDGE system involves using
content planning rules to decide what to say, and dialogue planning rules
to manage interactions with the user. The discourse plan built up as a
result of the planning process is used in dealing with interruptions and
in recovering from misunderstandings.

In the last chapter we described the content planning rules and the
basic planning process. In the remainder of this chapter we will describe
the main dialogue planning rules, how the system deals with misunderstandings, how it treats interruptions, and how the rules are use in
conjunction with content planning to generate an interactive explanation. The planning rules have been developed in the first instance for
managing *tutorial* explanatory dialogues. However, the chapter will conclude by briefly discussing how they can be adapted for different types
of discourse.

4.4.1   The Main Dialogue Planning Rules: Structuring Se-
quences of Exchanges

The EDGE dialogue planning rules have two (overlapping) functions: to
control interactions and to decide on aspects of the presentation (such as
the use of meta-comments and discourse markers). The latter aspect was
introduced in the last chapter (section 3.4.4). This chapter will therefore

```
d-plan informing.transaction (content-goal)
    subgoals: d-goal boundary.exchange (content-goal 'open)
              d-goal teaching.exchanges (content-goal)
              d-goal boundary.exchange (content-goal 'close)

d-plan teaching.exchanges (content-goal)
    subgoals: call plan-content (content-goal)
```

Figure 4.1
Informing Transaction Rule

complete the description of the rules by showing how they may be used to control interactions. This first section will focus on the main rules, which are used to structure basic sequences of exchanges with the user.

These rules are based on a modified version of Sinclair and Coulthard's model of classroom discourse [SC75], simplified so that it is appropriate for one-to-one interaction. About 20 dialogue planning rules were developed, with a working subset given in appendix B.2.

The Transaction: High Level Dialogue Structure   As we saw in chapter 2, Sinclair and Coulthard proposed a hierarchical model of dialogue structure based on five levels. The top level was the *lesson*, which we will not be concerned with here. The next level was the *transaction*, which corresponded roughly to a discussion of some topic or instruction in some task. The remaining levels were the *exchange, move,* and *act*. We will use the transaction, and in particular the *informing* transaction, as the top level dialogue planning rule in the EDGE system.

The *informing transaction* rule describes how a discussion of a topic begins with an opening boundary exchange, involves a number of teaching exchanges on the topic, and ends with a closing boundary exchange. The basic rule was introduced in section 3.4.4, and is repeated in figure 4.1. The figure also illustrates the *teaching exchanges* rule which results in content planning being initiated, so that the content of the teaching exchanges can be determined.[3] This is done simply by putting the relevant content goal on the agenda.

---

[3]Note that the goal type *call* in the second rule is used to invoke a lisp function — in this case the function *plan-content*.

The basic informing transaction rule is used to plan opening and closing sequences around the main explanation topic. However, other discourse sections also have characteristic openings and closings. We therefore define two other types of transaction — the *sub.transaction* for inserting opening statements at the beginnings of subtopic discussions (as discussed in the last chapter), and the *interrupting.transaction* for planning opening and closing markers and meta-comments around interruptions. The interrupting transaction is discussed in section 4.4.3.

Opening and Closing Exchanges The form of the opening and closing boundary exchanges used to begin and end discussions of some topic will in general vary according to the roles of the participants. Where the roles are equal the form of the exchanges is such that the participants have the opportunity to jointly agree to start or end the discussion. However, in the dialogues studied in chapter 2 the role of the expert was usually such that they had the right to determine alone the topic of the discussion.[4] The opening exchange was therefore often simply a statement of what was about to be explained. The expert was also normally responsible for ensuring that the novice understood the explanation. The closing sequence therefore provided the novice with the opportunity to continue the dialogue if they still didn't understand.

The rules used to represent these basic opening and closing sequences are given in figure 4.2. The opening exchange, as we saw in the last chapter, simply involves a topic-opening discourse marker (*framing* move) and a meta-comment describing what is about to be explained (*focusing* move). The closing exchange is structured so that the system suggests closing an explanation of some topic, and the user acknowledges (discussed further later in this section). Opening and closing boundary exchanges are illustrated below:

Opening Exchange:

S: (framing move:) Right,
    (focusing move:) I'm going to explain how the light detector unit works.

Closing Exchange:

S: (suggest-close move:) Enough about how the light detector unit works?
U: (pupil-acknowledge move:) OK.

---

[4]This was in fact set by the experimenter and not open to discussion.

```
d-plan boundary.exchange (content-goal type)
   constraints: equal (type 'open)
   subgoals: d-goal framing.move (type)
             d-goal focusing.move (content-goal type)

d-plan boundary.exchange (content-goal type)
   constraints: equal (type 'close)
   subgoals: d-goal suggest-close.move (content-goal)
             d-goal pupil-acknowledge.move (content-goal)
```

Figure 4.2
Boundary Exchange Planning Rules

When the system is pausing, waiting for the user's acknowledgment, the user has the opportunity to ask follow-up clarification questions, thus extending the explanation. The structure of the dialogue is therefore not determined by the discourse grammar, but rather the structures defined (e.g., closings) provide opportunities for user initiative.

System-Initiated Teaching Exchanges The other major constituents of the basic theory are the teaching exchanges. In our model these will include both question-answer (*elicit*) exchanges, initiated by the system or user, and informing exchanges, initiated by the system. Exchanges initiated by the system are used to convey information or check on the user's understanding. Exchanges initiated by the user are assumed to be to find out some information. In this section we will focus on system-initiated teaching exchanges.

System-initiated exchanges result from subgoals in content planning rules, as we see in figure 4.3. A teaching exchange in a content planning rule causes control to shift to the dialogue planning rules, to select and plan the exchange. The content of the exchange (i.e., the proposition it concerns) will be specified as a result of content planning.

The goal of a system-initiated teaching exchange is for the system to have increased confidence that the user understands some proposition. This can best be satisfied either by informing the user of that proposition, or by asking the user a question which checks their understanding. If the system believes that the user does not already know the propo-

```
c-plan identify (device)
    subgoals: call pointat (device)
              d-goal teaching.exchange
                    ((list 'identify-wrt-diagram device))
    template: ("what" (ref device) "looks like."))
```

Figure 4.3
Example Content Planning Rule Involving a Teaching Exchange

sition, then it is best satisfied by telling the user that proposition. If the system already has some level of confidence that the proposition is known, then it should ask a question to check understanding.

If the system believes that the user definitely already knows the proposition, this does not mean that it can be left out of the explanation. As discussed in the last chapter, a statement may form a vital part of an explanation of some more complex concept — for example, the behavior of a complex device may be explained in terms of a sequence of simple known behaviors of components. If such a proposition is believed already known, then the system will simply inform the user of that proposition (rather than asking a question).

Based on these principles, a teaching exchange may be defined as follows:

```
d-plan teaching.exchange (fact)
    constraints: maybe-understood (fact)
    subgoals: d-goal teacher-elicit.exchange (fact)

d-plan teaching.exchange (fact)
    subgoals: d-goal teacher-inform.exchange (fact)
```

Note that the second planning rule has no constraints, but because the operators are ordered so the more specific versions are considered first, it will normally only be used if the proposition is *not* "maybe-understood" — i.e., if it is not understood or if it is definitely known. However, in both content and dialogue planning, there will sometimes be a whole set of operators which may apply. The unselected (less specific) alternatives may be used in replanning given some problem with the explanation.

The subgoals in the rules above refer to subtypes of system-initiated teaching exchange, rather than to lower ranks such as moves or acts.

The rest of this section will describe these two teaching exchanges in more detail, before moving on to describe the other types of teaching exchange allowed.

Teacher-Elicit Exchanges   A teacher-elicit exchange is defined in terms of its constituent moves:

```
d-plan teacher-elicit.exchange (fact)
    subgoals: d-goal teacher-elicit.move (fact)
              d-goal pupil-reply.move (fact)
              d-goal teacher-response.move (fact)
```

A teacher-elicit move consists simply of an elicitation act. An appropriate question template is obtained for the type of proposition concerned, and the question is presented to the user. A pupil-reply move consists of a reply act, and requires an answer from the user. Whenever the system is processing a goal that requires an answer from the user it will put up an appropriate menu. The menu items will include the alternative responses, plus options for avoiding or delaying answering a question. This latter option allows *insertion sequences*, where the user asks a clarification question before finally answering the original question. As we saw with closing exchanges, the dialogue planning rules are not prescriptive, defining ahead the structure of the discourse, as opportunities are provided for user initiative.

Once the user has replied the system will respond to their answer, using the teacher-response move. This has an internal structure of several linguistic acts (following [SC75]):[5]

```
d-plan teacher-response.move (fact)
    subgoals: d-goal teacher-assess.act (fact *answer*)
              d-goal teacher-evaluate.act (fact *answer*)
              d-goal teacher-comment.act (fact *answer*)
```

Depending on whether the answer is correct or not, this may result in statements like:

(1) Yes, very good, it's high.

(2) No, not quite, it's actually quite low.

---

[5]Note that the variable *answer* will have been set during the student's reply.

However, the *comment* act may result in a more complex remedial response, which is treated as an interruption, discussed in section 4.4.3 below.

Informing Exchanges and Acknowledgments   Informing exchanges consist of an informing move and an acknowledgment from the user. Acknowledgments provide a vital opportunity for the user to either indicate that they are following or interrupt with clarification questions.

In human verbal discourse, acknowledgments may be of many types. Sometimes one participant will explicitly pause, waiting for a verbal indication of understanding. However, eye movements and facial expressions may also be used to indicate understanding and acceptance of the other participant's contributions. And a lack of interruption at a *Transition Relevance Point* may also be viewed as an implicit acknowledgment (see section 4.1.2), though one supplying weak evidence of understanding.

In human-computer discourse it is difficult to capture this range of types of acknowledgment. It is not necessary to require a language-based response — clicking a mouse button, for example, may provide an acceptable acknowledgment. However, it does at least appear necessary to explicitly pause, waiting for the user's signal. In turn, the user is required to take an active step in acknowledging, rather than passively waiting for the system to go on. This leaves open the question of how often to pause. In the type of explanations that we are concerned with here it is appropriate to pause after every proposition conveyed. This is partly because the explanations are accompanied by graphical actions, discussed in chapter 6. However, alternative approaches may be easily defined by varying the discourse planning rules.

The definition of the informing exchange used in the EDGE system is given below. The *acknowledge* act causes the system to wait for the user to click the mouse button in the text window, or to click on "OK" in a set of fixed menu options.

```
d-plan teacher-inform.exchange (fact)
   subgoals: d-goal teacher-inform.move (fact)
             d-goal pupil-acknowledge.move (fact)
```

Asking What the Student Knows   The final type of exchange considered allows the system to ask the user directly if he or she knows some fact or topic. This type of exchange is not considered (as a distinct exchange type) in Sinclair and Coulthard's model. It occurs when the system has no direct or indirect information in the user model about whether that topic is known, and needs this to make a decision about how to explain. The form of this type of exchange is simple. The system asks whether the user knows the concept; the user replies with either "yes," "no" or "don't know"; and the system briefly responds (e.g., by saying "great" or "oh well").

User-Initiated Teaching Exchanges In a mixed initiative dialogue we obviously have to allow for user-initiated exchanges. If the roles of the system and user were the same we would want to allow the user to initiate the same types of exchanges as the system — asking questions, informing, and changing topic with boundary exchanges. However, in the EDGE system we currently restrict user initiative to asking questions. This is consistent with Sinclair and Coulthard's model of classroom discourse and allows a robust and practical system, but does not allow us to capture the range of styles of explanatory dialogue discussed in chapter 2. This limitation will be discussed further in chapter 7.

The user can ask a question (initiating a *pupil-elicit* exchange) at any point during the discourse when the system is pausing. For example, when the system is waiting for an acknowledgment after an informing or closing statement, or waiting for an answer after asking a question, then the user can interrupt with a question. As the question and its reply are viewed as an interruption (see section 4.4.3), the planned explanation will be resumed when the question has been satisfactorily answered. The reply to the question may be complex, resulting in a lengthy clarification subdialogue.

A pupil-elicit exchange has a simple form, consisting of a question from the student and a response from the teacher. However, things get a little more complex if the system has already planned to answer the question later in the explanation, so that the topic to be explained is already on the agenda (see chapter 3). The partial order of the agenda will indicate whether the question topic could reasonably be explained at the current point in the explanation, or whether there are prerequisite topics that should be explained first. In the former case the system removes the question topic from the agenda, then proceeds with answering the question. In the latter case the system suggests that the question is best answered later, and gives the user the opportunity to postpone the question.

In order to capture these different options the reply move has a relatively complex definition, including the following two rules:

```
d-plan teacher-reply.move (question-goal oldgoal)
    constraints: answered-later (question-goal)
    subgoals: d-goal postpone-question.exchange
                        (question-goal 'answered-later)

d-plan teacher-reply.move (question-goal oldgoal)
    subgoals: d-goal interrupting.transaction
                        (question-goal oldgoal)
```

The *oldgoal* argument is used to point to the goal that the system was pursuing when interrupted. The system uses this to work out what higher level goal the system was in the middle of executing. The *answered-later* function will examine the agenda to see if the question goal is already there. For example, at an early stage in the discourse the agenda might look like this:

```
d-goal teacher-inform.act
            ((causal-event LDR (light-intensity low) ...))
d-goal pupil-acknowledge.move
            ((causal-event LDR (light-intensity low) ...))
d-goal teaching.exchange
            ((causal-event LDR (light-intensity high) ...))
c-goal process (light-unit)
c-goal behavior (light-unit)
d-goal boundary.exchange ((how-it-works (light-unit)) 'close)
```

If the user asks at this point about the behavior of the light unit the system will note that this will be explained later anyway. If the partial order of the agenda indicated that it could be explained now, the answered-later function would remove the goal from the agenda, but return "false." In this case however the earlier goals on the agenda are concerned with explaining prerequisite material, so the function will return "true" and the discourse planner will initiate an *avoid-question* exchange. This involves telling the user why the question might be deemed inappropriate and asking if it should still be answered, for example:

S: I think that's better answered after I've finished explaining the light detector's structure. Do you still want it answered right now?

U: No.

The teacher-reply move has a transaction as a subgoal. This is one of several cases where a simple hierarchical discourse model, with ranks (such as *exchange* and *move*) invoked in a strict order, is inadequate to represent the complexities of dialogue control. A reply may consist of a single informing act, or a whole transaction on a new topic, and the content of that transaction may be negotiated with the user. However, the categories of transaction, exchange, move, and act still appear useful in providing a clear model which allows us to define conventional high level dialogue structures.

4.4.2   Recovering from Misunderstandings

The above rules provide the basic framework for structuring interactions with the user. However, equally important is how we can use the opportunities for interaction with the user to deal with any misunderstandings as the explanation progresses.

Such clarification or repair sequences can be categorized according to who identifies the misunderstanding and who initiates the repair. In simple clarification sequences the user identifies the problem and initiates the repair by asking a clarification question. These were discussed above, as part of the basic dialogue model. However, in some cases the user may be unaware of a misunderstanding, and it is the system which must identify the problem and initiate the repair. In the EDGE model this occurs when the user gives incorrect replies to *teacher-elicit* exchanges. The system must plan a response to correct the perceived misunderstanding. Yet another case to consider is where the user can recognize that they have some problem, but cannot identify the source of the misunderstanding. The user initiates the repair, but the system has to try to identify the problem.

In this section we will show how the EDGE system deals these last two cases — planning remediation sequences in response to a user error, and dealing with inarticulate repair initiators (where the source of the misunderstanding is not identified).

Opportunistic Tutoring and Remediation   If the user gives incorrect replies to the system's questions then the system may attempt to provide some remediation to enable to user to recognize *why* their answer was wrong. This is likely to be more effective in correcting misunderstandings than simply giving the user the correct answer. Such remediation responses are mainly used for *tutorial* dialogues, and have previously been analyzed and used in work on tutorial dialogue systems (briefly discussed in section 2.3). We use strategies based on work by Woolf and Murray [WM87], where information is given which should enable the user to work out why the answer given was incorrect. However, while Woolf and Murray define the strategies in terms of a transition network of options, we use the EDGE planning rule formalism.

Woolf and Murray's strategies include giving examples, giving hints or guidance, and discussing the consequences of the answer given. The strategies currently defined in the EDGE system are based on giving hints, based either on an analogy or on giving detail which should enable the user to work out the right answer. The strategies defined are specific to particular types of error, focusing on errors concerning the behavior of some device given some input value. An example remediation rule used in giving a helpful analogy is given below. The rule is considered when the user answers a question wrongly about a causal event concerning a particular device. It states that if the user knows the function of an analogous device, then the system should try comparing the functions of the two devices, say "so" (a summary marker act), and ask the question again.

```
r-plan event-reply (device inputs output)
   constraints: know-user ('function (device-analogy device))
   subgoals: c-goal compare-function (device
                                      (device-analogy device))
            d-goal marker.act ('summary)
            d-goal teacher-elicit.exchange
                   ((list causal-event device inputs output))
```

Remediation strategies are called from the *teacher-comment* act which is part of the *teacher-response* move discussed earlier. If the user has got an answer to a question wrong, and there is a response or remediation strategy which can be used for the particular type of error involved, then this act will cause an *interrupting* transaction to be called with the appropriate remediation goal as its argument. If there is no such strategy, then the act will cause the correct answer to be given. The following planning rule shows how the interrupting remediation strategy is called — the *response* function searches the set of possible remediation strategies to that type of fact for one that has all its constraints satisfied.

```
d-plan teacher-comment.act (fact answer)
   constraints: response (fact answer)
   subgoals: d-goal interrupting.transaction
                          ((response fact answer)
                *currentgoal*)
```

The default response to an incorrect answer (if there is no remediation strategy available) is to signal it incorrect, comment on the answer, and then give the correct answer. This is consistent with Murray and Woolf's remediation schema. However, as in their schema, preference is given to providing some more concrete remediation if that is possible.

Rules similar to those above were used in planning the following remediation subdialogue. This example is taken from the scripts of people using the system in the evaluation sessions, described in chapter 7:[6]

S: What's the output voltage (V2) of the heat detector unit going to be if its input heat intensity (H1) is high?

U: Low (0V).

S: Wrong, not quite,
OK, A heat detector unit is much like a light detector unit only:
– Its output voltage depends on the input light intensity.
– It has a thermistor instead of a light-dependent resistor.
This component here is a thermistor.
Let's go through what a thermistor does.
When the input heat intensity (H1) of the thermistor is high the output resistance (R1) will be quite low.
When it is low (cold) the output resistance (R1) will be quite high.
So, what's the output voltage (V2) of the heat detector unit going to be when the input heat intensity (H1) is high?

U: Quite high (toward 9V).

S: Precisely, very good, it's quite high (toward 9V).

The EDGE system does not attempt to provide a comprehensive set of remediation strategies — just to demonstrate how they can be incorporated into the basic framework. It would be possible to extend and clarify the approach by defining more general purpose remediation planning rules which could be specialized for particular types of errors.

---

[6]Note that a slightly earlier version of the system was used in the evaluation. Examples taken from these sessions may not always be fully consistent with the planning rules described in the text.

Guessing at the User's Problem Sometimes an explainee may recognize that they have failed to understand some explanation, but be unable to articulate exactly *why* they don't understand it. They may indicate the lack of understanding by a baffled expression, or by utterances such as "huh?" or "what?" The EDGE system attempts to deal with such cases, using the same framework as Moore [Moo89].

At any point when the system is pausing the user can indicate that they are confused by clicking on a "what?" fixed menu option. (This contrasts with Moore's system, where the user can only indicate confusion at the end of a planned explanation.) When the user indicates that they are not following, the system first attempts to guess at the source of this misunderstanding.

In order to guess at the source of the misunderstanding the system must represent in the discourse model the assumptions which have been made about the user's knowledge in planning the explanation. This information is in addition to the basic discourse structure information illustrated in figures 3.4 and 4.4. If the system has assumed that the user knows some essential background material, but this is not certain, it will hypothesize that the cause of the misunderstanding is the fact that this information is in fact not understood, and will offer to explain it.

If the system can't find a reason for the confusion it will simply attempt to explain the current topic another way. (This may be done by reexplaining any of the "ancestor" goals which led to the utterance preceding the indication of confusion.) In order to do this, when there is more than one way of explaining something the discourse model includes pointers to possible alternative subgoals. An example possible discourse plan node illustrating assumptions about the user and alternative plans is given below:[7]

```
Goal: c-goal structure (light-unit)
Parent-goal: c-goal how-it-works (light-unit)
Assumptions: know-user identity (light-unit)
Alternatives: c-goal compare-structure (light-unit heat-unit)
Subgoals: know-user components (light-unit)
          know-user function (light-unit)
```

---

[7]This example actually conflates information that will be in more than one node, but illustrates the basic approach.

Dialogue planning rules are defined for selecting the repair strategy
to be used when the user indicates confusion. Possible rules for finding
a suitable repair are given below:[8]

```
d-plan find-repair.exchange (content-goal)
    constraints: missing-background (content-goal)
    subgoals: d-goal system-suggest-problem.move (content-goal)
            d-goal user-repair-reply.move (content-goal 'background)

d-plan find-repair.exchange (content-goal)
    constraints: goal-alternatives (content-goal)
    subgoals: d-goal system-suggest-alternatives.move (content-goal)
            d-goal user-repair-reply.move (content-goal 'alternatives)
```

The first dialogue repair rule above is involved in generating the following clarification sequence, where the system hypothesizes that the
user does not know what a thermistor does.

S: [...] then its output voltage is high.
U: What?
S: Don't you know what the thermistor does?
U: No.
S: Well, when the thermistor has a high input heat intensity its output resis-
    tance is quite low. When [...]

4.4.3   Dealing with Interruptions

In the EDGE system the clarification subdialogues resulting from misunderstandings are viewed as interruptions. They are not part of the
previously planned discourse, and that planned discourse is resumed
when the clarification is complete. In this section we will consider how
such interruptions are managed in such a way as to preserve the coherence of the discourse.

When the dialogue resulting from a particular discourse goal is to be
regarded as an interruption, the *interrupting transaction* dialogue rule
is used to plan appropriate opening and closing statements around the
subdialogue. These are vital, as if an explanation is resumed without

---

[8]The *user-repair-reply* move will result in a *repair* variable being set which can
be accessed by the rule which actually does the repair.

the subdialogue being "closed" it will not appear coherent. A discourse marker may sometimes be used to indicate the beginning of an interrupting sequence, but the way an interruption is closed and the preceding discourse resumed is of more interest. For short interruptions a simple discourse *pop* marker ("anyway") may be used, resulting in sequences like the following:

"Well, the light intensity is high so the resistance is low. Anyway [...]"

However, for longer interruptions more work is required. One way of resuming from a long interruption is with a meta-comment like:

"Anyway, we were in the middle of explaining how the light detector works."

Another way commonly used in verbal explanations is to repeat part of what was said before the interruption. The following example is taken from the transcripts of verbal expert-novice explanations:

E: Each of these acts rather like a switch, so if this is high..
N: You say shorted back to base, but there's a capacitor?
E: Right, there is indeed, come to that in a sec.
   Each of these is acting like a switch, so if this voltage here is high, this will turn on.

In order to provide appropriate meta-comments and repetitions the system must be able to determine what it was in the middle of doing. For this, the discourse model must be examined. In the EDGE system the discourse model includes a complete representation of the explanation plan so far. An example discourse plan for the content of an explanation was given in figure 3.4, while a discourse plan including dialogue actions is given in figure 4.4. The plan represents the intentional structure of the discourse, with the arguments to goals providing a primitive model of focus [GS86]. Because we are concerned with tutorial discourse it is also similar to the curriculum plans discussed by Murray and others [Mur89], as the intentional structure is based on subtopic and prerequisite relations between the concepts being explained.

The discourse plan given in figure 4.4 illustrates the state of the discourse after the opening exchange and one informing statement (identifying the light unit). The system is awaiting the user's acknowledgment of this first inform. As in figure 3.4, bold typeface indicates goals which are not fully expanded (or planned out), but are on the agenda, representing an outline plan of the future discourse.

In our simple model of focus the items on the "focus stack" correspond to the arguments of the "ancestor" goals of the current goal. In the example discourse plan these are:

```
(how-it-works (light-unit))
light-unit
(kind-of light-unit potential-divider)
```

The objects in focus include the current proposition being expressed (kind-of ...), the main object being talked about (the light unit), and the plan corresponding to the currently focused discourse segment (the plan to explain how the light unit works). This latter plan will be an argument to a *transaction* discourse goal. More distant ancestor goals will be less salient than recent ones. This corresponds fairly well with Grosz and Sidner's proposals for attentional state.

The discourse plan is used as follows to find out which goal the system is in the middle of pursuing. The plan must be examined to find which ancestor goals of the next goal on the agenda led to utterances in the previous discourse section, before the interruption (corresponding to the *oldgoal* in the interruption rule below). The lowest such goal in the tree is the one the system should say it was in the middle of doing. To find such a goal requires an explicit plan-based discourse model — a tree representation of the whole discourse, rather than a list of propositions uttered or a stack of goals.

Interruptions are structured by defining an interrupting transaction. The basic form of the interruption is defined as follows:

```
d-plan interrupting.transaction (content-goal oldgoal)
   subgoals: d-goal boundary.exchange (content-goal 'push)
             d-goal teaching.exchanges (content-goal)
             d-goal boundary.exchange (oldgoal 'pop)
```

In the current system the closing (resumption) boundary exchange normally involves a discourse pop marker such as "anyway" and a meta-

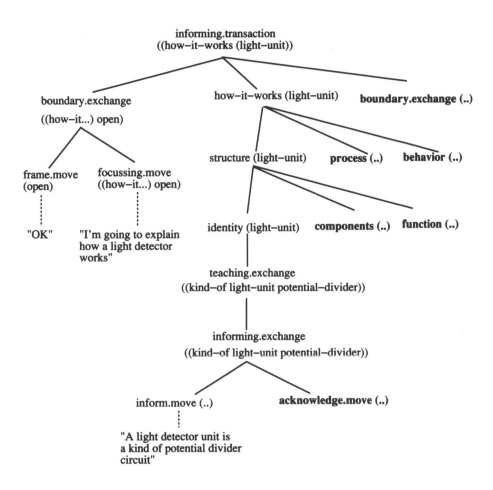

Figure 4.4
Example Partially Completed Discourse Plan

comment on the interrupted discourse (e.g., "Anyway, I was in the middle of explaining what the LDR does"). However, if the interruption came after a question the resumption will involve reasking the question. The following is an example dialogue section illustrating this sort of resumption (taken from the scripts of the evaluation session):

S: What's it going to be when the input light intensity (L1) is low?
U: What's a resistor?
S: OK, this component here is a resistor.
   Anyway, what's the output voltage (V1) of the light detector circuit going to be when the input light intensity (L1) is low (dark)?
U: Quite low (towards 0V).

Although remediation subdialogues and interrupting questions are both structured using the *interrupting* transaction, they are treated differently in the discourse model. The remediation subdialogue is not a true interruption — it shares an *intention* with a preceding discourse segment [GS86]. So though it interrupts the main flow of the explanation, the *attentional state* is treated exactly as if it were part of the main explanation. On the other hand, user questions do not necessarily share a discourse intention,[9] and will not be added to the main discourse model. By adding such interruptions only to the goal stack, and not to the main discourse model, a stack of discourse models is built up (as used by Litman and Allen [LA87] for discourse understanding), and items in focus will be restricted to those in the interrupting segment. When a discourse model is "popped off" the stack (as an interrupting sequence is completed) it is added to a list of past discourse segments, used when reasoning about previous discourse (e.g., to avoid repeating things which have been already been explained).

The discourse model obviously has many applications apart from dealing with interruptions. It provides a better basis for selecting referring expressions (e.g., pronouns); it allows the system or user to refer to the past discourse in terms of the discourse goals, for example asking for a repeat ("Can you explain what the light detector does again?") or mentioning that something has just been explained ("Well, we went through

---

[9]User questions **may** share an intention with the speaker (such as for the user to understand some information) — however, this intention may not be the immediately preceding one. Rather than attempting to work out what the dominating intention is, the system currently treats user questions as true interruptions.

that a minute ago"); and it allows the system to guess at problems and reexplain things when the user has problems with the explanation. However, this section should at least have shown how it is used for dealing with interruptions, and how it provides a simple and concrete representation of intentional and attentional structure similar to Grosz and Sidner's model.

4.4.4 Example Interactions: Integrating Content Planning and Dialogue Planning

In this section we will briefly discuss how particular interactions are planned in the context of the overall explanatory dialogue. Figure 4.5 illustrates a beginning section of an example explanatory dialogue, similar to the one in chapter 1. We will discuss how dialogue actions are selected below.[10] More comprehensive examples are given in chapter 6.

As we saw in section 3.2, the planning process begins by placing a goal such as the following on the agenda:

```
d-goal informing.transaction ((how-it-works (light-unit)))
```

The *informing transaction* rule is then used to expand this goal into a number of lower level goals — in particular an opening exchange, some teaching exchanges on the topic, and a closing exchange. The opening exchange is illustrated in utterance 1.

The *teaching exchanges* rule causes the system to place the actual teaching goal (how-it-works (light-unit)) on the agenda as a content goal, i.e.:

```
c-goal how-it-works (light-unit)
```

Content planning rules are used to determine how to expand this goal into primitive teaching actions, as discussed in chapter 3. Content planning results in teaching exchanges being initiated by the system. For example, utterance 2 results from the following teaching exchange:

```
d-goal teaching.exchange ((kind-of light-unit potential-divider))
```

In utterances 2–6, teaching exchanges result in simple inform statements (and acknowledgments), as the user is believed not to understand

---

[10]Remember that the system pauses after each numbered utterance. However, we do not show the user's acknowledgments.

S: 1. OK, I'm going to explain how the light detector unit works.

2. A light detector unit is a kind of potential divider circuit.

3. It has the following components:

4. – A fixed resistor.

5. – A light-dependent resistor.

6. This component here is a light-dependent resistor.

7. What do you think the light-dependent resistor's output resistance is when its input light intensity is high?

U: 8. High.

S: 9. No, not quite,

10. OK, a light-dependent resistor is much like a thermistor only:

11. – Its output resistance depends on its input light intensity and not heat intensity.

12. So, what do you think its output resistance is when its input light intensity is high?

U: 13. Quite low.

S: 14. Yes, very good, it's quite low.

U: 15. What does a fixed resistor do?

S: 16. Well, a fixed resistor always has a fixed output resistance.

17. Anyway, I was explaining what a light-dependent resistor does.

Figure 4.5
Example Section of Explanatory Dialogue

the given proposition. However, for utterance 7 the system believes that
the user *maybe* knows the proposition, so asks a question to check. This
pupil-elicit exchange results in a fairly complex dialogue sequence (utterances 7–14). First, after asking the question, the system has to obtain
an answer from the user. It does this by presenting a menu of possible
replies, and letting the user select an option. After obtaining an answer
the system provides some response or feedback. As the user's answer
is incorrect the system does this by looking for a possible remediation
strategy. In the example we assume that the user knows what a thermistor does, so it provides the feedback given in utterances 9–11. The
system resumes the previous discourse by asking the question again (initiating a new teacher-elicit exchange), obtains a correct reply (utterance
13), and gives some positive feedback (utterance 14).

At this point the user interrupts and asks what a fixed resistor does.
The system examines its agenda and looks to see if it is about to say that
anyway. In this case it isn't — the system had not planned to explain
the fixed resistor, believing it already known. The system therefore
replies, using the *interrupting transaction* to add appropriate markers
and resuming meta-comments.

4.4.5   Generating Other Types of Discourse

The above examples have been concerned with tutorial explanations of
simple electronic systems. However, the approach may be applicable to
other types of discourse and different domains. In the previous chapter
we hinted at how the content planning approach could be used to plan
tailored task descriptions or even simple stories. We can also extend the
dialogue planning rules so that dialogue actions depend on the roles of
the participants.

The roles and responsibilities of the participants influence the organization of opening and closing exchanges, and the occurrence of different
kinds of questioning exchange. In a non-tutorial role a *teacher-elicit* exchange is at least unusual. If the roles of the participants are more equal
then the choice of topic should be jointly determined, and the opening
exchange should have a different form. If the roles are completely equal
then the options available to the system and user should be the same
(though this is beyond the scope of the current system).

The EDGE system can generate role-dependent dialogue actions using
constraints on dialogue planning rules which access the current system

```
d-plan teaching.exchange (fact)
   constraints: role-allows-testing-questions (*system-role*)
                maybe-understood (fact)
   subgoals: d-goal teacher-elicit.exchange (fact)

d-plan teacher-inform.exchange (fact)
   constraints: role-pause-each-subtopic (*system-role*)
   subgoals: d-goal teacher-inform.move (fact)
```

Figure 4.6
Example Role-Dependent Dialogue Rules

role type, illustrated in figure 4.6. A simple hierarchy of role types is defined. *Tutorial* and *advisory* are subtypes of *information-giving*, while tutorial has more specific subtypes *formal tutorial* and *informal tutorial*. Each role definition specifies certain dialogue features (such as allowing testing questions, or having frequent pauses). The first rule in figure 4.6 simply prevents the system from asking *teacher-elicit* questions given certain role types. The second is one of a set of rules which enables a less interactive style of discourse, pausing only at the ends of transactions of different types rather than after every inform statement. Figure 4.7 illustrates a fraction of a dialogue given an advisory role. The assumptions about the user and the communicative goal are the same as for the dialogue in figure 4.5, so any differences are due to the different role. The system checks with the user before explaining topics, but pauses less frequently, and avoids teacher-elicit exchanges.

Changing the dialogue planning rules in other ways allows, for example, non-interactive explanations to be generated, explanations which only pause for user clarification questions at the end, or explanations which make more or less use of markers and meta-comments. The appropriate form depends on the application. However, separating content planning rules from dialogue planning rules, and allowing each to be influenced by flexible constraints, at least provides a basis for developing new types of explanatory dialogue system without reworking the whole set of rules. We have found no real problems with this separation, as the form of the dialogue appears largely independent of the details of its content.

S: 1. Right, I'll explain how the light detector works.

2. OK?

U: 3. OK.

S: 4. A light detector unit is a kind of potential divider circuit. It has the
following components:
– A fixed resistor
– A light-dependent resistor.
This component here is a light-dependent resistor.
Do you know what the light-dependent resistor does?

U: 5. Yes.

S: 6. OK.

Figure 4.7
Example Dialogue Section Given Advisory Role

Another way explanatory dialogues vary is in the degree of "risk"
taken in the explanation [Car92]. It is sometimes appropriate to assume,
in the absence of contrary information, that the user knows the background material and will interrupt if that is not the case. In other cases
a more careful approach is called for, checking what is understood, and
explaining where there is any doubt. The former approach may result
in a briefer explanation, but may also sometimes lead to confusion, and
a need for repair. Varying dialogues in this way requires a fairly minor
change to the way the content planning rules are interpreted. However,
doing this in a flexible way, so that the system can select which strategy
to adopt, is a more complex issue.

4.5   Conclusion

This chapter has shown how a dialogue may be managed in a complex
explanation. Dialogue planning rules are used, both to provide the high
level organization of the dialogue and to deal with various types of local
response to user questions and misunderstandings. Allowing local responses makes the explanation more robust, as misunderstandings may
be cleared up as they occur.

The system has been influenced by a number of distinct approaches to discourse modeling. The overall framework is adapted from work in discourse analysis, concerned with the structure of tutorial discourse [SC75]. However, in operationalizing this model it was necessary to consider how to provide opportunities for user initiative within the framework. In this the model was influenced by work in conversation analysis, and the dialogue planning rules could probably be reworked in terms of the sorts of conversational rules used by Frohlich and Luff in their dialogue system [FL90]. In particular, we provide opportunities for repair or clarification after each utterance, and minimize the amount of advance planning of the discourse, so aspects of the local situation (focus plus assumptions about the user's knowledge) will influence each utterance, turn by turn.

The system has also been influenced by AI models of discourse (e.g., [GS86]). In particular, a hierarchical discourse model is maintained and used in selecting pronouns and in resuming the explanation following an interruption. Discourse markers are added using dialogue planning rules (largely based on [SC75]), and indicate intentional structure and interruptions [GS86]. As the intentional structure of the discourse is based around topic relationships these markers also indicate topic changes. Finally, work on tutorial dialogue systems has influenced how tutorial/remedial responses are structured.

These different ideas were combined with the goal of developing an effective and practical approach to generating interactive explanations, given the corpus of explanatory dialogues collected. Ideas from each area are combined in a reasonably clear and consistent manner, although the overall theoretical perspectives of the different fields are rather different.

The system succeeds, in a fairly simple and restricted way, in generating coherent, individualized, responsive, and robust explanations encompassing a range of dialogue phenomena, as discussed in section 4.3.2. Unlike most dialogue systems the system views the planning of an interactive explanation as an extension of planning a non-interactive explanation. Dialogue is not viewed as a sequence of short monologues, but rather dialogue and monologue are described in the same framework. The content of a dialogue may have the same overall coherent organization as a monologue (or text), while a monologue may be interactive as far as there is at least the possibility of user interruption.

Overall then, the EDGE model provides a practical example of how flexible explanatory dialogues may be planned and generated. The next chapter will complete the framework, discussing how the user model may be updated as the discourse progresses, and summarizing how this affects the discourse itself.

5 Updating the User Model

In the last two chapters we showed how an explanatory dialogue is planned in the EDGE system. A model of the user's knowledge of the domain influences this explanation in a number of ways. It influences the content of the explanation, for example by including background material if believed not already known, and it influences the choice of dialogue actions, for example by asking questions to check on the user's knowledge.

In this chapter will will discuss how such a user model may be obtained. A rough model of the user's knowledge may be available prior to the explanation. However, this initial model will normally be crude and inaccurate. It is therefore important to be able to update this model as the explanatory dialogue progresses. By continuously updating it we can both form a more accurate picture of the user's knowledge and also respond to actual changes in their knowledge resulting from learning (or forgetting). The resulting improved model can be used to better tailor the rest of the explanation.

The chapter will begin with a discussion of the general issues involved in user modeling, before presenting the EDGE user modeling component. This component uses information gathered from the normal interactions with the user to update stereotypical knowledge about their understanding of the different concepts in the domain.

5.1 Issues in User Modeling

User modeling in general is extremely complex. There are numerous types of information about the user which may be relevant to the system's task, and many ways this information may be gathered. In this work we will only be concerned with information about the user's *knowledge* gathered through a normal *dialogue* with the user.

The user's knowledge can be represented in a number of ways. The simplest approach, and the one we will use, is to represent the user's knowledge as a subset of the expert's (i.e., the system's). For each concept in the domain the system can represent its belief concerning whether the user knows that concept. An early system to use this approach was the Scholar system [Car70], which tagged each concept in the domain as believed known or believed unknown. This basic approach has become known as *overlay* modeling, as the student's knowledge is represented as an overlay of the expert's knowledge. The overlay approach to user modeling is limited as it both fails to explicitly represent the user's possible misconceptions, and does not allow for the possibility that the user may have useful knowledge and beliefs that conflict with or differ from the system's. However, the approach provides a practical basis for limited, but useful, user modeling and has been used in a large number of systems. Further approaches to user modeling, especially with respect to dialogue systems, are discussed in [KF88, KW89].

Building up and maintaining a model of the user's knowledge is difficult for two main reasons. First, we have only very restricted information to work with. From a few clues, taken from direct interactions with the user, we have to be able to fill in the picture, guessing at the rest of the user's knowledge. Second, our assumptions about the user's knowledge will be continually changing. This is partly because the user's knowledge will actually be changing, and partly because all our deductions about their knowledge are uncertain and liable to be revised in the face of more reliable or recent information. Dealing with such changing assumptions is in general a difficult problem, requiring techniques for non-monotonic and uncertainty-based reasoning.

The following sections will be concerned with these issues. The first will show how detailed user models can be built up given restricted information, and the second how consistent sets of assumptions can be maintained in the face of changing information.

5.1.1 Guessing What the User Knows

Information about the user can be built up in a variety of ways. At the beginning of any user-system interaction the system may have information derived from previous sessions with that user, or default information based on the user's class (or stereotype). As the interaction progresses this initial model can be updated based on direct inferences from the user's input and the system's statements, and indirect inferences, where partial information about the user's knowledge is used to make further guesses about what is and isn't understood [WK89].

User modeling using stereotypes is based on the fact that users in particular classes tend, by default, to have particular attributes. If we have information about the user's class we can therefore guess at certain attributes. This approach was pioneered by Rich, who developed a system which could recommend books, based on a limited self-description

provided by the user [Ric79]. This description was used to guess at
the user's class or stereotype, which was then used to guess at their attributes (as relating to book preferences). This knowledge was in turn
used as the basis for book selection. For example, a particular word
used in their self-description might suggest that they belonged to the
stereotype *feminist*, which might in turn suggest that they are likely to
like science fiction books.

Rich's approach requires that a great deal of work is done in setting up
the system, encoding the typical attributes of a whole set of stereotypes.
When we are only concerned with the user's knowledge of the domain
(rather than their general attributes) a simpler approach is possible. The
stereotype(s) assigned to the user can be based on their level of expertise in some domain. Then, rather than representing the set of concepts
normally understood by users at each different expertise level, we can
assign difficulty levels to each concept in our domain model, corresponding to the level of expertise at which it is normally first understood. We
can then assume that if a user has a level of expertise greater than this
difficulty level then that concept is likely to be understood. This approach was used by Wallis and Shortliffe in generating explanations for
the Mycin expert system [WS85]. Each rule and concept in the knowledge base was tagged with its difficulty (or complexity). Then, based
on the expertise level of the user, rule trace explanations were tailored
so as not to use concepts believed unknown to the user.

The basic approach of using levels of expertise can be extended by
using knowledge of the relationships between concepts in the domain
to make further inferences about the user's knowledge. Sleeman, for
example, in his User Modelling Front End (UMFE) system [Sle85], used
knowledge of general/specific relationships between concepts. Inference
rules were defined, stating for example that if a concept was known then
its parent concept was also probably known. The system would ask
the user a small set of questions at the beginning of a session, and fill
in knowledge about their understanding of different concepts by using
knowledge about their likely level of expertise, plus inference rules based
on these conceptual relations.

The UMFE system did not address the issue of how to update this
kind of model as the session progressed. Each interaction with the user
is a potential source of information about their knowledge and understanding, and should be used in verifying and revising an initial user

model. Chin addressed this issue, using a rough model based on the user's level of expertise and updating and refining this through natural language dialogue with the user [Chi89]. For example, if the user asked a question, the system could deduce that they probably didn't know the answer, but did know any presupposed information in the question.

Kass and Finin present a more exhaustive set of indirect inference rules which may be used to update a user model in a natural language dialogue [KF87]. These include rules based on principles of communication, the structure of the domain knowledge, and the actions performed by the user. The domain knowledge rules are extensions of the sorts of rules used in the UMFE system, while the action rules relate knowledge of what the user is doing in the dialogue to knowledge of the skills and procedures they may be using (and therefore know). The communicative rules are inspired by Grice's maxims for communication [Gri75], and include assuming that an utterance by the user will be considered (by the user) to be relevant to their goals and contain sufficient and non-ambiguous information.

Kass's inference rules were all based on the principle that a user model could be built up simply by "looking over the shoulder" of the user. The user modeling component did not need to take any active steps to find out information about the user. Kass showed just how much could be achieved by such a passive approach. However, in human dialogues (especially tutorial dialogues) people do sometimes ask direct questions about the hearer's knowledge (e.g., figure 2.8 in chapter 2). Practical systems should infer as much as they can from "normal" interactions with the user, but be able to ask direct questions when this is required. If such questions are asked, then they should be asked at the relevant point in the dialogue and not ahead of time, so that the discourse does not appear incoherent to the user.

5.1.2   Dealing with Uncertainty

Any approach to user modeling has to consider how to represent uncertain information and deal with changing and conflicting assumptions. This is a general problem and research area within artificial intelligence, with many key papers in [SP90]. In this section we can only show what the problem is, and discuss the solutions which have been adopted within the user modeling community.

The first issue to consider is what to do when there is conflicting information concerning whether the user knows some concept. For example, their level of expertise may suggest they know it, but their last question suggests they don't. Two approaches have commonly been used to deal with this. Either rules for updating the user model are ordered in some way, so more certain rules are always considered before less certain (and the less certain information ignored), or numerical weights are assigned both to rules and to facts in the user model. The latter approach has the advantage that all information, certain and uncertain, contributes to the model, but it is unclear how to combine the different weights appropriately.

The second (and related) issue is how to revise the rest of a user model when one part of it is changed. A change in part of the model may invalidate other parts of the model as inference rules may have used the old data to indirectly derive new assumptions. If the inference rules are applied whenever new data is added to the user model (forward chaining) then this means that the justifications for facts in the user model must be explicitly maintained, and some kind of reason maintenance system (e.g., [dK86]) used to update the user model. This approach has been used by Huang et al. [HMGN91]. However, a simpler approach is to use the inference rules by backward chaining when the system needs to know if the user understands some concept. Then if the "base" assumptions about the user change, any derived assumptions will implicitly change too. The GUMS system [Fin89] essentially takes this approach, using a default logic to deal with the conflicting inferences.

5.1.3 Summary: Criteria for a Simple User Modeling Component

From the above discussion we can see that a user modeling component for a dialogue system should be able to use a number of different sources of information in order to derive (or rather, guess at) what the user knows, and deal appropriately with conflicting and changing assumptions. The system should be able to use the normal interactions with the user as the main basis for updating and refining the user model, but be able to fall back on the direct strategy of asking the user whether they know something.

The main sources of information which can be used to update a user model (and which are used in the EDGE system) are:

- What the user says and asks.
- What the system tells the user.
- The user's level of expertise.
- Relationships between concepts in the domain.

These different sources of information are ordered above according to their (approximate) reliability. For example, the system should trust information derived from what the user actually says more than it trusts information based on the user's assumed level of expertise. The system should be able to deal with these preferences, and maintain a consistent model of the user's knowledge.

5.2   The EDGE User Modeling System

The EDGE user modeling component allows a model of the user's knowledge of the domain to be built up and updated as an explanatory dialogue progresses. The component is integrally linked with the discourse planning component, so the information in the user model is just that which is needed by the discourse planner, and the actions taken in the dialogue enable the user modeling component to obtain this relevant information.

We will first describe the way the user's knowledge is represented in the user model, and the way the system uses different sources of information to update this model. This will be followed by a reminder of the different ways the model affects the discourse, and an example showing how the user model is updated and used in a short fragment of an explanation.

5.2.1   Representing the User's Knowledge

The representation of the user's knowledge is based on an overlay model on the topics and subtopics in the domain. These topics and subtopics are effectively defined by the content planning rules used to explain them. For example, if there are planning rules for explaining how a device works and for explaining a device's function, then the user model will represent the user's knowledge of both these types of topic. Of course, the planning rules are for explaining general types of topic (such as how a device works), while we represent the user's knowledge of particular instances of these topic types (such as how a light detector works). The planning rules used to explain types of topics make explicit the

subskill and prerequisite relationships between them. This knowledge
enables us to make inferences about the user's knowledge based on conceptual relationships. The rules effectively define a hierarchy of concepts, from the most general (e.g., "How a light detector circuit works"
or "How to make cookies") down to the most specific (e.g., "What the
resistance of an LDR is when the light intensity is high" or "How to
chop chocolate in a food processor"). The system represents the user's
knowledge both of the general, high level topics, and of the detailed,
low level topics. This is vital for planning an explanation. It's no good
just knowing whether the user knows detailed concepts when making
high level decisions about explanation strategies, yet these details are
important for lower level decisions.

So, given a particular type of topic (such as a device's behavior given
a particular input value), the user modeling component reasons about
and represents the user's knowledge of particular instances of that topic,
based on particular values for the arguments of the associated planning
rule. For example, the planning rule *causal-event*, used to describe the
behavior of a device given a particular input, has three arguments: the
device being described and the relevant input and output values. The
user model will therefore contain entries like the following:

```
causal-event:
   (light-unit (light-intensity high) (voltage lowish))   known
   (light-unit (light-intensity low) (voltage highish))   maybe-known
   (heat-unit (heat-intensity high) (voltage lowish))     unknown
```

The system distinguishes between those concepts which the system is
confident that the user knows, and those about which it is less certain
(based, for example, on indirect inference). These are indicated by the
labels *known* and *maybe-known* above. The system may also believe a
concept *unknown* or be *undecided* about whether it is known or not.
These labels provide a very simple representation of the degree of belief a system has concerning a user's understanding of some concept.
Although simple, the four distinctions were found to be adequate for
making rational decisions in planning an explanation, and could be updated in a reasonably principled manner. Because a user model is only a
rough guess at the user's actual knowledge, more complex schemes (e.g.,
using numerical weights and rules for combining evidence) were viewed
as inappropriate.

5.2.2   Building and Updating the User Model

The initial user model is based on the user's claimed level of expertise, plus indirect inferences based on relationships between concepts in the domain. This initial model is updated based on more direct evidence from the interactions with the user. This more direct evidence may also cause the user's level of expertise to be revised, which may result in a more major change in the model (where the assumptions about the user's understanding of many concepts may change).

The system deals with conflicting and changing information in a fairly simple manner. Direct inferences based on interactions with the user cause an immediate change in the representation of the user model, overwriting anything that was there before. This is seen as acceptable as recent information based on user-system interactions is likely to be more reliable than anything there before (especially as the user's knowledge is continually changing). The direct inference rules used are summarized in figure 5.1. Indirect inferences based on the user's level of expertise and conceptual relationships (figure 5.2) are only applied when the system needs to know whether the user knows some concept. Once the system has deduced this, it does *not* record the information explicitly in the user model. This may occasionally be inefficient, but also circumvents the need for a reason maintenance system — if deduced information was recorded in the model, it would be necessary to also record all the assumptions on which it was based, and revise the model when these assumptions changed.

The indirect inference rules are applied in order, and only when there is no direct information in the user model. More reliable inferences are considered before less reliable, and less certain information ignored when better evidence is available. This avoids consideration of conflicting information, aiming only at a best guess at what the user knows based on the most certain current information.

Most of the inference rules in figures 5.1 and 5.2 should require no discussion. However, the use of difficulty levels and expertise is a little more complex. In the EDGE electronics explanation system, four levels of expertise are defined. These are:

Novice: Knows no electronics and virtually no electricity.

Beginner: Remembers electricity from school, but no electronics.

Dialogue Exchange	Inference
System tells user X, User acknowledges	User maybe knows X
System asks user X, User replies correctly	User knows X
System asks user X, User replies incorrectly	User doesn't know X
System asks user if she knows X	(Whatever user's reply is)
User asks X	User doesn't know X

Figure 5.1
Direct Rules for Inferring What User Knows.

Condition	Inference
All subconcepts known/unknown	Parent concept known/unknown
All subconcepts known or maybe known	Parent concept maybe known
Concept difficulty greater than level of expertise of user	Concept unknown
Concept difficulty less than level of expertise of user	Concept maybe known
Parent concept known or maybe known	Subconcepts maybe known
Parent concept unknown	Subconcepts unknown

Figure 5.2
Indirect Rules for Inferring What User Knows

Intermediate: Knows a little electronics.

Expert: Knows a fair bit of electronics.

These are given numerical values (1–4) for convenience. Difficulty levels may be defined for any of the concepts in the domain. For example, a transistor's behavior might be familiar to someone who knows a little electronics, so has difficulty level 3. Most features of a resistor will have difficulty level 2, while how an astable multivibrator works will have difficulty level 4. If the user is of intermediate level of expertise it is therefore likely that they will know all about resistors, and unlikely that they will know how an astable works. However, it is less clear whether they will know what a transistor does.

The following example illustrates the representation of difficulty levels for the behavior of different devices. The difficulty of "the behavior of the light detector unit" is 2, while that of the NAND gate is 4.

```
behavior (device)
    difficulty: (((light-unit) 2) ((NAND) 4))
```

As the discourse progresses, it may be necessary to revise the user's assumed level of expertise. For example, if the user correctly answers a number of difficult questions, or asks about a number of easy concepts, then this suggests that the level of expertise given may need to be revised. The EDGE system therefore accumulates a difficulty rating based on the concepts asked about and the questions answered. When the user correctly answers a question, then the difficulty value of the associated concept is added to the total rating. When the user incorrectly answers a question, or asks a question, then one less than the difficulty level of the concept is added to the total rating. The user's expertise level is based on their initial claimed expertise level and on the difficulty rating. The expertise level is initially given a certain weighting, depending on its likely reliability, and this weight is incremented each time the difficulty rating is updated. The expertise rating at a later point in the dialogue is based on the following:

$$\frac{initial.expertise.level \times initial.weighting + total.difficulty.rating}{current.weighting}$$

Suppose the initial expertise level was 2, with weighting 5. After a user correctly answers a question of difficulty 4, the rating would be $(2 \times 5 + 4)/6$. If a user then incorrectly answers a question of difficulty 2, the new rating would be $(2 \times 5 + 4 + 1)/7$. The increased weighting represents the increased evidence for the expertise level, and gives the system inertia while still allowing it to revise the level. The actual expertise level used is in fact the expertise rating rounded to the nearest integer. This tends to avoid conclusions about what the user knows based on a marginal difference between their believed expertise level and the difficulties of concepts.

5.2.3   Using the User Model

So far we have seen how a model of the user's knowledge is built up as an explanatory dialogue progresses. As we saw in chapters 3 and 4, this model is used to make various choices concerning what to say or ask in that dialogue. The model is used to influence both the content of the discourse and the choice of specific dialogue actions.

The user model is used to make three main types of decision about discourse content. First, it is used in the selection of the appropriate strategy to teach a concept (in particular, when to use an analogy). Constraints on content planning rules refer to the user model, and are used in rule selection. Second, it may be used to decide on the level of detail of a causal explanation. This again uses constraints on the content planning rules. Finally, it is used to decide what background (or optional) information to include. This background material will be represented as preconditions on the content planning rules, and only included if not already believed known.

The user model influences the choice of dialogue actions in two ways. First, the system uses the model to decide whether to teach some fact by simply informing the user, or by asking a testing question. As the aim of the system is to increase its certainty that the user knows the fact, it will ask a testing question when it is uncertain but believes the fact may be known. If it believes that the fact is unknown, little will be achieved by testing the user, so the system simply informs. If it believes the user definitely knows the fact (but the fact needs to be presented, as part of an argument) it again simply informs the user, as repeated questioning about known material would be tedious and counterproductive.

Second, the user model will influence when the system asks the user directly whether they know some topic. This will occur when the system needs this information to make a discourse planning decision, but the user model cannot provide it. This might occur when the user's assumed level of expertise makes it borderline as to whether the topic would be known, and there is no other information.

5.2.4 Example

Full annotated examples of explanatory dialogues are given in the next chapter. However, a short example will be discussed here, illustrating how the user model is updated and used. Again, we will use an example based on the type of dialogue given in chapter 1. The fragment below results from the goal of explaining what a light-dependent resistor does, given no initial information about whether this is already known. We will show how the user model both determines and is determined by the utterances in the dialogue.

S: Do you know what a light-dependent resistor does given different inputs?
U: I think so.

S: Well, we'd better go through it to check. What do you think its output resistance is when its input light intensity is high?

U: High.

S: No, not quite, it's actually quite low.
What do you think its output resistance is when its input light intensity is low?

U: Quite high.

S: Yes, excellent, it's quite high.

Initially the system needs to know whether the user knows what a light-dependent resistor does. Unusually it has no information available, as the expertise level of the user is the same as the difficulty level of the concept, so it asks a direct question:

S: Do you know what a light-dependent resistor does given different inputs?

U: I think so.

The user's answer causes the concept (what a light-dependent resistor does) to be explicitly marked as maybe known. As it is not definitely known the system's response is to go through it anyway:

S: Well, we'd better go through it to check.

Explaining what a light-dependent resistor does involves the two sub-goals of explaining what it does when the input light intensity is high, and explaining what it does when this is low. To select the appropriate teaching exchanges to use to explain these subconcepts the system needs to know whether the user may already know them. The system infers that the user maybe knows the subconcepts, as they have said that they think they know the "parent" concept. The system therefore asks a question to check the user's knowledge:

S: What do you think its output resistance is when its input light intensity is high?

U: High.

S: No, not quite, it's actually quite low.

The user answers incorrectly, so momentarily the system marks the subconcept as unknown. However, the system corrects the user, so it then marks the subconcept as maybe known. The system goes on to test the user's knowledge of the second subconcept.

S: What do you think its output resistance is when the input light intensity is low?
U: Quite high.
S: Yes, excellent, it's quite high.

Now the subconcept (what the LDR does when the light intensity is low) is marked as known. The other subconcept is still marked as only maybe known.

There are a number of possible problems with the inferences illustrated. For example, it could be argued that once the user has got the question relating to one subconcept wrong, the system should assume that the user does not know the other subconcept. Or that correcting the user after an incorrect answer should not lead to the assumption that the user now maybe knows the correct answer.

The rules and preferences used in the current system are not definitive, and should be revised following further empirical evaluation. The important thing is that an increasingly detailed model of the user's knowledge may be built up and used without destroying the coherence of the discourse.

5.2.5 Issues and Extensions

The user model inference rules used in the EDGE system could be developed and extended in various ways. These include extending the range of inferences that are made on the basis of the user's utteraces; extending the range of indirect inferences made on the basis of domain relations; and extending the representation of the user model itself, beyond a simple overlay of domain concepts.

The range of inferences made on the basis of user utterances could be extended if the utterances were allowed in unconstrained natural language rather than menus. Then some of the strategies suggested by Chin [Chi89] and Kass and Finin [KF87] could be adopted. These include assuming that the user knows all the presuppositions of an utterance. If, for example, the user asked what sort of component a transistor was, the system could at least infer that the user knew that the transistor was a kind of component.

The range of inferences made on the basis of domain relations could be more easily extended. Currently the system uses subskill relations between types of concept in the domain (e.g., understanding a *process* involves understanding all the individual *causal-events*). These are very general kinds of relations, and do not include particular relations between objects in the domain. A more comprehensive user modeling component could use domain object relations such as *specialization* and *part of* to make more complex inferences. For example, if the user knows the behavior of a particular type of NAND gate, it is reasonable to suppose that they know the behavior of all NAND gates if they can identify them as such.

However, to develop a more principled user modeling component we should consider in more detail *why* the different domain-based inference rules are valid. In general, a rule may be valid either because a user should be able to infer the hypothesized concept from the given one, or because a user would be unlikely to have learned the given concept without prior knowledge of the hypothesized one. As an example of the former, the user should be able to infer a device's behavior given knowledge of the behavior of its components (and general circuit knowledge). As an example of the latter, a user is unlikely to have learned how a complex circuit works without knowledge of simple electrical concepts like resistance and voltage. In order to make effective use of these different types of domain-based inference, a user modeling component should be based on theories of human plausible inference and learning.

The representation of the user model itself could be extended in a number of ways, such as allowing misconception recognition, or representing user goals as well as beliefs. Both these extensions would in turn require techniques for inferring and updating such models, and techniques for using such models to influence the generation of the explanation.

Misconceptions might be based on overall "buggy" models of circuit behavior, or on more local incorrect beliefs which lead in turn to incorrect deductions. As an example of the latter, if a user had incorrect beliefs about the behavior of some component, their conclusions about the behavior of circuits involving that component would probably be wrong too. A system should be able to hypothesize underlying causes of errors and confusions, and address these causes rather than surface manifestations. Remediation and repair should again be linked more clearly to models of human inference and learning, extending approaches such as McCoy's [McC89].

Inferring a user's underlying information-seeking goals could be attempted using more detailed stereotypes (with associated default goals), verified or updated on the basis of the user's question-asking behavior. These goals could then be used in tailoring the explanation more appropriately, possibly using ideas from McKeown's work on tailoring advisory explanations given an inferred user goal [McK88], or from the Berkeley UNIX consultant project [WCL+88]. It is unclear how this would apply in the "how things work" domain, but in a system which provided extended explanations about how to use certain computer commands, for example, inferring the user's current task and underlying goal might prove very important.

Finally, as well as considering the different ways in which the user modeling component could be extended, we should consider how it should be revised for different types of discourse. For example, for non-tutorial discourse it is inappropriate to ask "testing" questions. When the system is uncertain about the user's knowledge it should ask whether they know something, rather than testing them by setting a question to be answered, as disussed in chapter 4.

5.3   Conclusion

The EDGE user modeling scheme is an extended overlay model similar in many ways to the UMFE system [Sle85] and to Chin's KNOME system [Chi89]. It allows assumptions about the user's knowledge to be updated as an explanatory dialogue progresses. These are just rough guesses about the user's knowledge. An interactive explanation system does not demand correct knowledge about the user, but approximate knowledge may improve its performance. The criteria for a user modeling component discussed in section 5.1.3 are satisfied, with the system using direct and indirect rules of inference for updating the model, and maintaining a consistent model in the face of varying and changing sources of information.

The user modeling component is integrally related to the explanatory dialogue planner itself. A variety of inference rules are used based on the different types of interaction in the system, and all the user model information required may be obtained in the context of a coherent discourse. The user model representation is based on existing conceptual structures in the discourse (content) planning rules, allowing concepts to be represented at various levels of abstraction — those levels needed by the application system.

The main limitations of the approach are related to the limitations of overlay modeling in general. Misconceptions are not explicitly represented (though the remediation strategies may be directed at addressing some particular misconception), and the system assumes that the user's relevant knowledge is a subset of the system's. It further assumes that the user's goal is to increase their knowledge in line with the system's. Although these assumptions are not valid in general, they allow a simple and practical framework for updating and using a user model, appropriate for generating user-sensitive explanatory dialogues in a range of applications.

6 Application and Examples: Explaining How Circuits Work

The previous three chapters have shown how general principles have been used in developing the EDGE model of explanatory discourse. This model is applicable to a range of domains and to a range of discourse types. However, as well as general principles we need to look at the particular problems of generating explanations in a particular domain. In this chapter we will therefore focus on the problems of generating explanations of how simple electronic systems work. This domain is sufficiently complex to provide a real test of the general principles involved, while presenting new, more domain-specific problems.

We will start by discussing some of the particular problems and issues involved in explaining how things work, before going on to describe in detail the particular domain models and content planning rules used in explaining circuit behavior. These models and planning rules are used in generating simple model-based explanations including both graphical and textual actions. The chapter will end with extensive annotated examples of explanations generated by the system.

6.1 Explaining the Behavior of Physical Systems

In order to develop an effective explanation system in a particular domain it is helpful to look at the underlying domain models that can be used to reason in that domain, how human experts construct explanations in that domain, and how novices learn, forming new conceptual structures in that domain.

Early work on generating explanations of the behavior of physical systems focused on the underlying device models and the reasoning processes involved. De Kleer, in his early work on *qualitative reasoning*, showed how qualitative models of circuits could be developed which could be used with a qualitative reasoning system to generate causal explanations of a circuit's behavior [dK84]. Qualitative reasoning systems are concerned with the qualitative (rather than exact, numeric) behavior of systems. Variables in the system are assigned *qualitative values*, based on *intervals* in some *quantity space*. For example, a variable such as temperature could be assigned the value $(0, T1)$ where $T1$ is some significant temperature (e.g., a boiling point). Its derivative in that interval could be assigned the value $(0, \infty)$, or "+". Given a set of values such as this, and some *qualitative differential equations* defining the relations between variables, a qualitative reasoning system could deduce the possible qualitative time-dependent behaviors of the system, and from this could construct a causal explanation.

A number of people have shown how such qualitative models may be combined with a graphical simulation, to generate a combined graphical and textual explanation which can be used in teaching [FS81, Sim85, WF86, FF88]. White and Frederiksen [WF86] focused on how student learning could be facilitated by presenting them with increasingly complex types of qualitative model, starting from simple, non-time-dependent ones. Falkenheiner and Forbus [FF88] showed how explanations of fairly complex systems could be obtained, by representing the system at different grain sizes, and using simplifying assumptions about its working.

Qualitative reasoning systems (of certain types) can be used to generate simple causal explanations based on an underlying device model. However, human explanations are much more varied and complex than this. Stevens and Steinberg showed that human explanations of physical systems varied along a number of dimensions [SS81]. They classified a large number of explanations in Navy training manuals and came up with a typology of explanation types observed:

Behavioral: Describing the input-output behavior of the system.

Physical-causal: A causal explanation based on the physical decomposition of the system.

Synchronous: Describing equilibrium states and behavior.

Information flow: Describing information propagated in a system.

Stuff-state-attribute: Describing state or attribute changes.

Stuff-as-a-transport-medium: Describing how some "stuff" (e.g., water) is used to transport something such as energy.

Componential: Describing the components of the system.

Topological: Describing components and connections.

Geometric: A more quantitative description of structure.

Stevens and Steinberg suggest that this enumeration of explanation types may be based on four main distinctions. These are *structure vs. mechanism, individuated vs. aggregate events/components, qualitative* vs. quantitative, and *external vs. internal properties*. They acknowledge that in practice a combination of more than one type of explanation may be appropriate, suggesting that instructional goals might include things like: "To describe a reducing valve, use one physical-causal explanation at the level of the first set of subcomponents, and one behavioral explanation; but to describe a venturi, use one aggregate objectifying individual molecular events and one stuff-state-attribute with energy objectified."

At this point Stevens and Steinberg's work begins to sound somewhat like the independent work on text generation by McKeown and Paris [McK85, Par88] (described in chapters 2 and 3). Both classify types of explanation or utterance and show how a complete description may be structured from several types. Stevens and Steinberg give a more detailed classification of explanation types, and suggest that different types of device will need different types of explanations. McKeown classifies single utterances in a more domain-independent way, and attempts to obtain general schemata which may be used to generate descriptions in a wide range of domains.

From these kinds of analyses (and that presented in chapter 2) we can see that explanations of how things work are complex, involving structural and functional information as well as causal. Furthermore, causal explanations may be of many different types. However, human explanations, as well as including a wide range of types of utterance or description, also depend on the knowledge of the hearer. Paris claims that explanations for novices include mainly causal descriptions, while explanations for experts include mainly structural descriptions of a system [Par88]. Cox, on the other hand, suggests that explanations should take into account stages of learning development, and in particular the stages of understanding *figurative knowledge* involving the surface attributes and classification of the object(s); *cause-effect* knowledge involving causal relationships; *functional* knowledge (concerning the object's purpose); and *complex derivational* knowledge where results of actions may be derived [CJP88]. Each stage may only be understood once prior stages are understood. These early stages of understanding appear to come before Paris's expert level — only when the hearer has a good understanding of the derivational level is a simple structural or componential description adequate.

Miyake shows that for a complex system — in this case the workings of a sewing machine — it is insufficient to claim that people first learn the function, then the mechanism [Miy86]. In her experiments the process is shown to be iterative. Through a process of repeated negotiation and explanation people went through six levels of a *function-mechanism* hierarchy. At each stage they seek to understand a function assumed at the previous level. The process of understanding how something works is clearly far from simple. Explanations should reflect that process, and not be limited to a causal trace of device behavior.

The research summarized above suggests that explanations of how things work should have a number of features:

Structure of Explanations: Explanations should involve behavioral, causal, functional, structural, and identification/attribute information [SS81, McK85, Par88]. The types of information included should depend on the device being explained and the prior knowledge of the hearer [Par88, SS81], while the information should be ordered in such a way that the hearer can assimilate and understand the new information [CJP88], following the pattern of human expert explanations [McK85] (and chapter 2).

Levels of Explanation: Explanations should be given at different levels depending on the understanding of the student [Miy86]. It should be possible for the student to repeatedly ask "how does that work?" when given some behavioral description — though in practice there will always be some cutoff point where such explanations are too complex. Understanding may progress through a process of questioning and negotiation.

Graphics: Explanations should include graphical as well as textual actions [FS81, FF88, Sim85].

Qualitative Models: Explanations should be based on qualitative rather than numerical models [dK84, FS81]. However, in some cases the qualitative model may be quite simple (e.g., [WF86]). Ideally, different types of model should be available depending on the device being explained and the knowledge of the user [WF86, SS81].

The EDGE system is based primarily on the analysis of human explanations given in chapter 2, though informed by the principles given above. In the rest of this chapter we will describe in detail how the EDGE system is used to generate complex explanations of how circuits work.

6.2   The EDGE Circuit Explainer

For the EDGE system, generating explanations in a new domain involves writing a set of content planning rules for explaining concepts in that domain, and deciding on a representation for the underlying knowledge. This section will therefore discuss the content planning rules and the models developed for circuit explanations, before giving a number of annotated example explanations.

6.2.1   Planning Rules and Graphical Actions

In developing rules for explaining how things work we need to consider the overall structure of the explanation, the way the explanation depends on the user's knowledge, and the way graphical actions can be incorporated in the explanation. These points will be discussed in turn, both extending and summarizing the discussions in chapter 3. A more complete working subset of the content planning rules used is given in appendix B.1.

Structuring the Explanation   In chapter 2 we observed that explanations of circuit behavior tend to have the following organization:

- First, the circuit is *identified* as an instance of a particular sort of circuit.
- Next, any *components* may be described, including their individual *behaviors* given different inputs.
- Next, the *function* of the circuit may be given.
- Next, the *process* or causal sequence of *events* (explaining the overall behavior) is given.
- Finally, the overall *behavior* is summarized.

We have argued that the *identification*, *component*, and *function* descriptions may be regarded as *background* material, enabling the main *process* to be better understood. (They are viewed here as aspects of a description of the *structure* of a device.) Identifying the device as an instance of a known class provides an initial link into the student's knowledge, while knowledge of the components makes it easier to follow the description of the process or causal sequence of events. Finally, explainin g a device's function motivates interest and provides expectations concerning its overall behavior. Figure 6.1 shows the two rules used to achieve this

```
c-plan how-it-works (device)
   constraints: device-structure (device)
   preconditions: know-user structure (device)
   subgoals: d-goal sub.transaction
                   ((c-goal process (device)) 'open)
             d-goal sub.transaction
                   ((c-goal behavior (device)) 'summary)
   template: "how" (ref device) "works"

c-plan structure (device)
   constraints: device-type (device)
                know-user ('structure (device-type device))
   preconditions: know-user identity (device)
                  know-user components (device)
                  know-user function (device)
   template: "what" (ref device) "is like"
```

Figure 6.1
Top Level Content Planning Rules for Explaining How Circuits Work

high level structuring (repeated from chapter 3).[1]

From these two simple rules it should be clear how the explanation is structured to include different types of utterance and how the content will depend on the hearer's knowledge. The identity, components, and function will only be described if not believed already understood. If, for example, the user is believed to be familiar with the device's class and function but not with one of its components, then just that component will be described before going on to explain how the whole circuit works.

Further planning rules are defined for explaining the identity, components, function, process, and behavior of a device. The first two are simple. The *identity* rule looks for a parent class believed known to the user, and results in an utterance or question concerned with identifying the device as an instance of that class. The *function* rule describes the device's function in terms of how its output value depends on its input value (e.g., it provides an output voltage which depends on its input light intensity). These rules are given in appendix B.1.

---

[1]See chapters 3 and 4 for a discussion of the planning rule representation and the use of the *subtransaction* goal type.

```
c-plan components (device)
   constraints: device-components (device)
   preconditions: know-user constituency (device)
                  forall comp in (device-components device)
                              (know-user component (comp))
   template: "what" (possref device) "components do."

c-plan component (device)
   preconditions know-user identify-diagram (device)
               know-user behavior (device)
   template: "what" (ref device) "does"
```

Figure 6.2
Content Planning Rules for Describing Components

The *components* rule lists the components in the system, and describes each (if not already known), while the individual *component* rule identifies the component on the diagram (discussed below) and gives its behavior.

Causal Behavior   The most important part of an explanation of how something works is arguably the description of the causal processes involved.   The EDGE system derives the sequence of causal events explaining the circuit's overall behavior using a simple qualitative model of the circuit.   If a component in the model is changed, the explanations generated will therefore also automatically change.

In general, developing and using qualitative models is a complex problem in itself.   We avoid addressing these problems by concentrating on a class of electronic circuit where the behavior is very simple.   The behavior of these systems can be explained as a function of the input-output behaviors of the components — no feedback or time-dependent behavior is involved and each device has a single significant output value.   Larger circuits may be viewed as composed of a number of simpler circuits and explained in terms of their input-output behavior.   This approach is based on a recent electronics textbook [Joh87].   The models required for this approach are very simple.   However, they are sufficient for us to show how a text planning system can base part of its explanation on an underlying qualitative model.

Figure 6.3 illustrates the main planning rules used to explain causal processes. The first rule effectively states that knowing the *process* of a device involves knowing the causal sequences resulting from different input values. The second states that knowing a causal sequence involves being told what input value is being considered, and the causal sequence of events resulting from that input. The rule also includes a graphical action (discussed in the next section) so that the input value will be illustrated in the diagram. The third rule has a subgoal which calls a special interpreter whose job it is to generate the causal steps of the explanation at the highest level of detail. This interpreter uses a simple model of the device's structure and deduces the sequence of input-output events that make up its behavior for a given input value.

Each such causal event will then be explained to the user. The causal event planning rules are written so that the event given may be explained at different levels of detail, depending on constraints on the user model. [2] If the event concerns the input-output behavior of a subcircuit, and that circuit is believed not familiar to the user, then the system will explain the behavior in terms of more detailed component behaviors.

When the system describes a high level step in the causal explanation, the student always has the opportunity to ask for a more detailed explanation. Thus the explanation of a complex system may progress through interaction with the student (as suggested by Miyake [Miy86]).

The causal explanations involve *qualitative* values. Because of the simplicity of the example circuits it is not necessary to do complex reasoning about intervals. The following values/intervals are used:

Low: 0 V, 0 Ohms etc.

Quite Low: The interval (0, 4.5 V) or (0, 1 KOhm).

Average: 4.5V, 1KOhm.

Quite High: (4.5, 9 V) or (1, ∞ KOhm).

High: 9 V or infinite resistance.

These were the sorts of values used in most of the human explanations. The associated intervals are only given to show that the underlying

---

[2]In fact, an extra type of causal event rule is needed, to prevent events being explained in detail in other inappropriate contexts.

```
c-plan process (device)
   constraints: device-structure (device)
   preconditions: forall inputs in (device-input-values device)
                             (know-user causal-sequence
                                        (device inputs))
   template: "how" (ref device) "works given different inputs."

c-plan causal-sequence (device inputs)
   subgoals: d-goal teaching.exchange
                  ((list 'initial-state device inputs))
               call display-value
                     ((first inputs)
                      (first (device-input-meters device)))
               c-goal event-sequence (device inputs))
     template: "how" (ref device)
                 "works given the following inputs:" inputs

c-plan event-sequence (device inputs)
   subgoals: forall event in (deduce-events device inputs)
                     (c-goal causal-event
                             (event-device event)
                             (event inputs event)
                             (event-output event))
```

Figure 6.3
Content Planning Rules for Explaining Causal Behavior

reasoning is still sound. For example, if a potential divider has one quite high resistance (near the 0V rail) and one quite low one (near the 9V rail) the output voltage will be quite high. If it has one quite high one and one low one the output voltage will be high. The "average" resistance of 1KOhm is defined arbitrarily.

Graphical Actions The EDGE system incorporates a simple approach to generating graphical actions within an explanation, similar to the more recent approach developed by Maybury [May91a]. Any planning rule may involve graphical as well as linguistic actions, with special functions defined to implement the different graphical actions. Communicative goals are typically satisfied by a combination of both graphics and text, each reinforcing the other.[3] The system does not reason about which medium is more appropriate for some given content, or how graphical and textual decisions impinge on each other [WAGR91, FM90].

Graphical actions are currently implemented as Lisp calls. Functions are defined for pointing at given objects, and displaying iconic representations of input and output values. The rules in figure 6.4 illustrate how such actions are invoked, while figure 6.5 illustrates the actual output of the system when these two planning rules are used in an explanation of the light detector unit.

The "devices" passed as arguments in these plans are particular device instances, such as a particular light-dependent resistor. These instances are illustrated in a displayed diagram and have input and output meters where their input and output values may be displayed. They are produced at the beginning of a session from the underlying device model, as the diagram is created. The underlying device models will be discussed in the next section.

In order to coordinate the text with the graphics, utterances in the text must reference labels in the diagram. In particular, the names of different input and output values (e.g., V1, H2) are indicated on the associated meters and accessed (via the device instance) in sentence templates. For example, the lisp call (`meter-label (device-output-meter device)`) could be used to access the name of the output value used on the diagram, allowing descriptions of values such as "the output resistance (R1)."

---

[3]Graphical actions were implemented on a now obsolete computer, so are not fully supported in the most recent version of the system.

```
c-plan identify-diagram (device)
    subgoals: call pointat (device)
              d-goal teaching.exchange
                    ((list 'identify-wrt-diagram device))
    template: "what" (ref device) "looks like."

c-plan causal-event (device inputs output)
    constraints: equal ((length inputs) 1)
    subgoals: call display-value
                    ((first inputs)
                      (first (device-input-meters device)))
              d-goal teaching.exchange
                    ((list 'causal-event device inputs output))
              call display-value (output
                                  (device-output-meter device))
    template: "what the output of" (ref device)
              "is when its inputs are:" inputs
```

Figure 6.4
Graphical Actions in Planning Rules

As well as generating graphical output, the system allows the user to point at the diagram to provide a context for their questions. When the user clicks (with the mouse) on a particular region of the diagram a menu of appropriate questions is displayed. This allows the user to ask questions using the diagram (rather than the text) as the context, as occurs in human explanatory dialogues in this domain.

6.2.2   Device Models

The planning rules discussed above take particular devices as arguments. These are instances of generic device types, and inherit properties from the generic object. For example, a plan to describe a component may have a particular light-dependent resistor as its argument (say LDR6). This will have a position (so it can be pointed at), input and output meters which are used to indicate values, and, when appropriate, pointers to component instances. It will inherit its other properties from the general light-dependent resistor definition.

At the beginning of an explanation, if the device named has not been

"This component here is a light-dependent resistor."

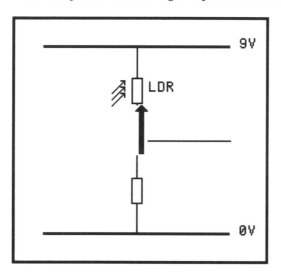

"When the light-dependent resistor has a high input light intensity (L1) its output resistance (R1) is quite low."

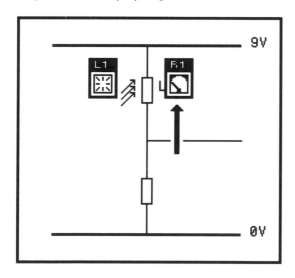

Figure 6.5
Graphical and Textual Output in Circuit Explanations

explained before, the system will create a diagram from the structural
description of the device and routines for drawing components. At the
same time it will create object instances for the device, its subsections
(if there are any), and all its components. This is managed so that input
and output meters (and labels) correspond, so a device which takes its
input voltage from the output voltage of another device will share that
meter. The new structural description based on the component instances
is used as the new *structure* property of the device instance, so that
when components are described or a causal description given using that
description, all the appropriate component instances are used. Similarly
a list of the component instances is formed and used as the *components*
property of the instance. The construction of the diagram also causes
different *active regions* of the graphics window to have attached questions
menus, as discussed in the previous section.

Before a new device type may be explained, it is necessary to define
its structure, type, typical inputs, *black box* behavior, and so on. This
is done using definitions such as the one in figure 6.6. This definition
indicates that typical input values for this circuit are high or low heat
intensities; that it is a kind of potential divider circuit; that its output
value (given particular inputs) may be determined using the function
heat-unit-output; that its components are a fixed resistor and a thermistor; and that its structure is such that its behavior is determined as a
function of a general potential divider circuit's behavior, taking its input
(resistance) values from the output of the fixed resistor and thermistor.
The function *heat-unit-output* must be defined, so that the behavior of
the device can be simply obtained given different input values.

Larger circuits may be built up of smaller ones, defining the structure
as a function of smaller circuit sections. For example, the *heat warning circuit*, explained in some of the examples below, has the following
structure definition:

```
Model heat-warning
     structure: (lambda (heat)
                   (lamp-unit (inverter (comparator
                                          (heat-unit heat)))))
```

This description indicates that the circuit takes a single value *heat* as
its input, and its behavior is a function of the behavior of four circuit
sections: a heat unit (defined in figure 6.6), a comparator, an inverter,

```
Model heat-unit
    name:              "heat detector unit"
    input-values:      ((heat-intensity high))
                       ((heat-intensity low))
    type:              potential-divider
    output-function:   (function heat-unit-output)
    components:        fixed-resistor
                       thermistor
    structure:         (lambda (heat)
                            (potential-divider
                                (fixed-resistor) (thermistor heat))))
```

Figure 6.6
Defining a Heat Detector Unit

and a lamp unit.

In the EDGE system fourteen device models have been defined, allowing explanations of five circuits (each consisting of simpler circuit sections or components). The circuits modeled were taken from the electronics textbook mentioned earlier [Joh87]. More sophisticated device models would be required to represent the full range of circuits in the text book, where more complex time-dependent, feedback behavior was involved. However, the representation is sufficient to represent a fairly wide range of simple circuits, and allows us to test the basic approach, where complex graphical-textual interactive explanations may be generated based on a simple underlying domain model.

6.2.3 Example Explanations

This section will go through a number of detailed examples of explanatory dialogues generated in this domain, showing how the user model, content planning rules, and dialogue planning rules are used in conjunction. In each case the dialogues are generated by the system with the author acting as student.

The aim of this section is to give an overview of how a complete explanation is generated. Examples of specific types of interactions such as interruptions and remediation sequences were given in chapter 4.

Explaining How a Light Detector Works   The first detailed example is an explanation of how a *light detector* unit works. Initially the user model is set so that the system believes:

- The user knows what type of circuit a light detector unit is.
- They don't know what its components are or what its function is.
- They know what a fixed resistor does, but only maybe know exactly what a light-dependent resistor does when it is light.
- They know what a potential divider circuit is.
- They don't know the behavior of the light detector unit.

Figure 6.7 shows the complete resulting dialogue, given an initial call to give an *informing transaction* of how the light detector works.[4]   A large amount of reasoning is involved in generating each utterance of the explanation.   Figure 6.8 shows a trace of the goals called by the discourse planner in generating the introductory comment and the first statement, and describes what is inferred about the user's knowledge.[5] The first column displays the current goals and plans of the system (a trace generated by the system). The second includes the actual dialogue in quotes, and comments on the inferences being made in italics.

It is worth noting a number of things in these examples. The dialogue planning rules have been used to generate discourse markers and meta-comments at the beginning of the topic and major subtopics, as well as to structure the exchanges with the user. The user modeling component motivates certain questions (e.g., utterance 7) and causes assumptions about the user's knowledge to be updated. Near the beginning of the dialogue the system infers that the user knows what the LDR does, and therefore doesn't ask any more questions about this in the remaining dialogue. If the same explanation was given again it would not explain the behavior of the LDR at all and would ask a question about the light detector's function. If this question was answered correctly it would infer that the student now knew the *structure* of the light detector.

Explaining Other Circuits   Almost all the examples in this book have been from explanations of how this simple light detector circuit works. However, the same planning rules may be used to explain a range

---

[4] As in the other examples, menu calls have been replaced with text.
[5] The example is simplified slightly so that the device's constituents are presented in a single utterance.

S: 1. OK, I'm going to explain how the light detector unit works.

2. It has the following components:

3. – A fixed resistor.

4. – A light-dependent resistor.

5. This component here is a light-dependent resistor. *Points at LDR.*

6. What do you think its output resistance (R1) is when its input light intensity (L1) is high?

U: 7. Quite low.

S: 8. Correct, excellent, it's quite low.

S: 9. The light detector's function is to produce an output voltage which depends on its input light intensity.

10. Right, Suppose its input light intensity (L1) is high.

11. When the light-dependent resistor has a high input light intensity (L1) its output resistance (R1) is quite low.

12. What do you think the fixed resistor's output resistance is?

U: 13. Medium.

S: 14. Yes, very good, it's medium.

15. When the potential divider circuit has one quite low input resistance (R1) and one medium input resistance (R2) then its output voltage (V1) is quite high.

16. Suppose the light detector unit's input light intensity (L1) is low.

17. When the light-dependent resistor has a low input light intensity (L1) its output resistance (R1) is quite high.

18. The fixed resistor always has a medium output resistance.

19. When the potential divider circuit has one quite high input resistance (R1) and one medium input resistance (R2) then its output voltage (V1) is quite low.

20. So, When the light detector unit has a low input light intensity (L1) its output voltage (V1) is quite low

21. When it has a high input light intensity (L1) its output voltage (V1) is quite high.

22. Enough about how the light detector unit works?

U: 23. OK.

Figure 6.7
Explaining How the Light Detector Unit Works

d-goal informing.transaction ((how-it-works (light-unit14)))	*An informing transaction starts with a boundary exchange.*
d-goal boundary.exchange ((how-it ..) open)	*This is simply expanded as follows:*
d-goal framing.move (open)	
d-goal marker.act (open)	"Now, "
d-goal focusing.move ((how-it..) open)	
d-goal meta-comment.act ((how-it..) open))	"I'm going to explain how the light detector circuit works."
d-goal teaching.exchanges ((how-it..))	*Start planning content to teach how light detector works.*
c-goal how-it-works (light-unit14) know-user structure (light-unit14) c-goal structure (light-unit14)	*As the user is believed not to know the "structure," a content goal is set to explain this.*
know-user identity (light-unit14)	*But the type of device is known, so don't explain this.*
know-user components (light-unit14) c-goal components (light-unit14) know-user constituency (light-unit14)	*The constituents aren't believed known, so these are explained.*
c-goal constituency (light-unit14)	

d-goal teaching.exchange
    ((components-of light-unit14
        (resistor11 LDR12)))
	The constituency goal causes a teaching exchange to be initiated.

d-goal inform.exchange
    ((components-of light-unit14
        (resistor11 LDR12)))
	An informing exchange is selected as the user probably doesn't know this.

d-goal inform.move
    ((components-of light-unit14
        (resistor11 LDR12)))	

d-goal inform.act
    ((components-of light-unit14
        (resistor11 LDR12)))
	"It has the following components:
	– A fixed resistor
	– A light-dependent resistor."

d-goal pupil-acknowledge.move	
d-goal pupil-acknowledge.act	Student clicks on "OK." *System now infers user may now know what a light detector's components are.*

Figure 6.8
Detailed Trace of First Few Utterances of a Dialogue

of circuits, and could be generalized to explain how other physical devices worked. In this section we will therefore give examples of explanations of how two more circuits work: an inverter, which is another simple circuit similar to the light detector unit, and a low heat warning circuit, which is a more complex circuit mentioned in section 6.2.2. The low heat warning circuit switches a lamp on when the temperature drops below some set threshold value. The relevant circuit diagrams and models are given in appendix B.5.

In the first example (figure 6.9) the system starts off with no knowledge of the user except that they only knows a little about electronics. The system can therefore only use difficulty levels to guess whether concepts are known. Two direct questions are asked about what the user knows. These are asked at the appropriate point in the dialogue, when the system needs to know whether the user knows some background knowledge. Comments are again in italics.

The second example (figure 6.10) shows how a causal explanation may be given at different levels of detail depending on the user's assumed level of understanding, on interrupting questions from the user, and on problems with answering system questions. Again, the system starts with relatively little knowledge of what the user knows, but gains some information from a few questions. To shorten the example we assume that the user already knows the behavior of a comparator. As with all these examples, dynamic graphical actions are important, but hard to represent in a static diagram. Figure 6.11 illustrates the display at one point in the explanation.

6.3   Conclusion

This chapter has shown in detail how the EDGE discourse planner may be used to generate explanations in a particular domain — explaining how simple electronic systems work. This involved developing explanation planning rules based on analysis of human explanations and on related research on explaining physical systems. A simple representation for device models was also discussed, which enabled causal explanations and graphical actions to be generated for new devices with little associated overhead. A number of detailed examples were given, showing how each aspect of the system — content planning rules, dialogue planning

S: 1. OK, I'm going to explain how the inverter works.
Do you know what it is like? *The difficulty levels for what an inverter is like and what a potential divider circuit is are set to the novice electronics level, so direct questions are asked.*

U: 2. No.

S: 3. Well, Do you know what a potential divider circuit is like?

U: 4. Yes.

S: 5. Great, An inverter is a kind of potential divider circuit.

6. It has the following components:

7. – A fixed resistor.

8. – A transistor.

9. This component here is a fixed resistor.

10. What do you think its output resistance is?

U: 11. Average (1KOhm).

S: 12. Yes, very good, it's average (1KOhm). *The system now infers that the user definitely knows what the fixed resistor's "behavior" is.*

13. This component here is a transistor. *The system assumes that the user probably doesn't know that much about transistors, as they are quite difficult.*

14. When it has a high input voltage (V1) its output resistance (R2) is low.

15. When it has a low input voltage (V1) its output resistance (R2) is high. *The system now infers that the user may understand what a transistor does.*

16. The inverter's function is to provide an output voltage that depends on its input voltage.

17. OK, Suppose its input voltage (V1) is high (9V).

18. What do you think the transistor's output resistance (R1) is when its input voltage (V1) is high? *Because the user may understand about transistors now, the system asks a question to check.*

U: 19. High.

S: 20. No, that's not right, it's low (conducting). *System now infers that student doesn't know the transistor's behavior for a high input voltage. The dialogue then continues in similar manner to the one in figure 6.7*

Figure 6.9
Explaining the Inverter Given Uncertain Information About User's Knowledge

S: 1. OK, I'm going to explain the behavior of the low heat warning device. Do you know what it is like?

U: 2. No.

S: 3. Well, Do you know what a warning device is like?

U: 4. Yes.

S: 5. Great, A low heat warning device is a kind of warning device.

6. It has the following components:

7. – A lamp unit.

8. – A inverter.

9. – A comparator.

10. – A heat detector unit.

11. This component here is a lamp unit.

12. What do you think its output brightness is when its input voltage (V7) is high? *Note that the system uses the difficulty level of the lamp (1) to make the assumption that the user probably knows what it does.*

U: 13. High.

S: 14. Yes, great, it's high.

15. What do you think its output brightness is when its input voltage (V7) is low (0V)?

U: 16. Low.

S: 17. Yes, splendid, it's low. *The system now infers that the user knows about the lamp.*

S: 18. This component here is a inverter.

S: 19. When it has a high input voltage (V5) its output voltage (V7) is low.

20. When it has a low input voltage its output voltage (V7) is high.

U: 21. How does the inverter work?

S: 22. Well, Suppose its input voltage is high.

23. When the transistor has a high input voltage (V5) its output resistance (R4) is low.

24. When the potential divider circuit has one average input resistance (R3) and one low input resistance (R4) then its output voltage (V7) is low.

25. Suppose the inverter's input voltage (V5) is low (0V).

26. When the transistor has a low input voltage (V5) its output resistance (R4) is high.

Figure 6.10
Explaining a Complex Circuit (continued on next page)

27. When the potential divider circuit has one average input resistance (R3) and one low resistance (R4) then its output voltage (V7) is high.

28. Anyway, I was in the middle of describing the components of the low heat warning device.
    This circuit section here is a comparator.

29. This circuit section here is a heat detector unit.

30. When it has a low input heat intensity (H1) its output voltage (V2) is quite high.

31. When it has a high input heat intensity (H1) its output voltage (V2) is quite low.

32. The low heat warning circuit's function is to produce an output brightness that depends on the input heat intensity.

33. Right, Suppose its input heat intensity is low.

34. What do you think the heat detector's output voltage (V2) is when its input heat intensity (H1) is low?

U: 35. Quite high.

S: 36. No, not quite,
    OK, The fixed resistor always has a medium output resistance.

37. When the thermistor has a low input heat intensity (H1) its output resistance (R2) is quite high.

38. The fixed resistor always has a medium output resistance.

39. When the potential divider circuit has one quite high input resistance (R1) and one medium input resistance (R2) then its output voltage (V2) is quite low. *System explains in more detail, because of user incorrect response.*

40. So, What do you think the heat detector's output voltage (V2) is when its input heat intensity (H1) is low?

U: 41. Quite low.

S: 42. Yes, very good, it's quite low.

43. Anyway, I was explaining what the low heat warning circuit's components do.
    When the comparator has a quite low input voltage (V2) its output voltage (V5) is low.

44. What do you think the transistor's output resistance (R4) is when its input voltage (V5) is low? *System starts to explain inverter in detail, as it hasn't yet concluded that user probably understands this.*

Figure 6.10
Explaining a Complex Circuit (cont.)

"When the inverter has a high input voltage (V5) its output voltage (V7) is low."

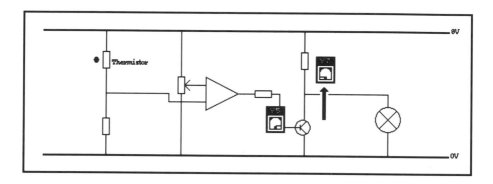

Figure 6.11
Graphical Display in a Complex Explanation

rules, and the user modeling component — combine to enable complex explanatory dialogues to be generated.

We have shown that explaining how things work involves much more than simply presenting a qualitative causal sequence of events. Many different types of explanation should be combined in order to generate understandable and effective explanations. The work integrates text planning approaches (such as [Par88]) with work on generating graphical-textual qualitative causal explanations (e.g., [FS81]). The underlying device models and causal reasoning processes are very simple, but it should be straightforward to use more sophisticated reasoning systems within the basic discourse planning framework.

7 Evaluation and Conclusion

In this chapter we will assess just how far the EDGE model provides an adequate framework for explanatory dialogue systems, and suggest areas for further work. The first section describes a limited empirical evaluation of the implemented system, as presented in the last chapter. The second discusses some of the limitations of the overall architecture. The final section summarizes the contributions of the model, including some possible practical applications.

7.1 Empirical Evaluation

Empirical evaluation is vital if we are to develop practical explanation systems. In our context it can serve two main purposes. First, it can be used in the development of the system, to refine and improve various *ad hoc* aspects based on feedback from the user. This type of evaluation is sometimes referred to as *formative* evaluation. Second, it can be used to assess the validity of the overall approach. This is appropriate once the main effort of system development is complete, and is sometimes referred to as *summative* evaluation.

For a practical system, both types of evaluation should ideally take place in the context or contexts that the system is meant to be eventually used in. This context includes the types of users testing the system, and their physical environment and activities. A system which is acceptable in a laboratory setting may not be so successful in a work context.

In a formative evaluation we aim to detect any problems with the details of the system, so that they may be corrected in later versions. Problems may be detected by monitoring the user's activities and obtaining their comments. Monitoring the user's activities may involve recording the session in various ways (e.g., video, tape, or computer log or script of session), or simply observation by the experimenter. Recording the session obviously has the advantage that later detailed analysis of system use is possible. The information recorded may include just the user-system interaction, or it may also include information about the system's internal state and reasoning.

Comments from the user can be obtained in various ways: by encouraging the user to talk aloud when using the system; by getting two users to use the system together and recording their dialogue; by going through some kind of questionnaire; or by interviewing the user.

Interviews with the user may be structured, going through particular points in turn, or unstructured, where the interviewer may elicit any information that appears relevant in the particular context.

For a summative evaluation we are more concerned with how the overall approach compares with alternative approaches, given some measure of performance. Measures of performance might include the amount of information that was learned, the efficiency at performing some task, or the usability of the system. Measures may be subjective (e.g., users saying they find this one easier to use than that one) or objective (e.g., measuring time taken to successfully perform a given task). Comparison with other approaches might involve side-by-side comparisons with competing systems, or comparison with published performance measures under well defined conditions. Alternatively "internal" comparisons may be done, by varying features of the system and seeing how this changes its effectiveness.

The EDGE system was not developed for a particular target set of users, so no attempts were made to evaluate it in a genuine operational context. The evaluation described here is primarily a formative evaluation, to suggest problems with the prototype system and ways they might be improved in later versions. We were therefore primarily concerned with the details of the system (such as the particular inference and planning rules used), rather than the overall approach. These "details" are vital for the development of a practical, usable system. Summative evaluation was limited to obtaining the subjective comments of users on different aspects of the acceptability of the system. Positive comments may at least suggest that the overall approach, based on an analysis of human verbal discourse, is worth pursuing. The rest of this section will describe the details of this evaluation, and the results and conclusions drawn. Further discussion of evaluation issues, particularly with respect to natural language systems, is given in [GJ92].

7.1.1   Details of the Evaluation

The evaluation was designed primarily to find out problems with particular aspects of the system, and in particular with the use of combined text and graphics, with the content of the explanations, with the dialogue, and with the user modeling rules. A simple task was set for a small number of subjects and various methods used to find out the problems in the different areas.

Task   The task the subjects were set was fairly open-ended. The subjects were asked to use the system[1] in order to find out how a set of circuits worked. They were told that there were four circuits that they could get explained, and how to start these explanations. They were all taken through one explanation to illustrate the basic mechanisms and facilities of the system. Then they were allowed to obtain any explanations they wanted until they felt they were familiar with the system and with the circuits. This typically took about half an hour.

Subjects   Eight subjects used the system. They were all members of the author's university department, so were not realistic potential users of the system. Their knowledge of the domain varied from complete novice to expert, though typically they had learned some electronics in the past, but did not remember it well.

Methods   The evaluation took place in two stages. The first was solely for system development and improvement (i.e., a formative evaluation). After each evaluation session (involving a single subject) the system was revised and debugged based on the problems exposed in the session. Three subjects were involved in this stage. The second stage, involving five subjects, was concerned also with the user's subjective view of the overall performance and acceptability of the system. However, at this stage we were still concerned with exposing further problems, so future implementations of the architecture may be improved.

The methods used in the evaluation were the following:

1. Recording the session: User-system interactions were logged by the computer as the session progressed. This was primarily in order to discover problems with the dialogue. Example extracts from the scripts obtained are included in appendix C, along with comments on some of the problems observed. The system's final user model (at the end of a session with a particular user) was also recorded, in order to discover problems with the user modeling rules. It could be compared with both the user's and the experimenter's assessment of the user's understanding.
2. Observation: Each session was observed by the experimenter, in order to discover problems with the basic use of the system, and in particular with the use of combined text and graphics.

---

[1]Note that the version of the system which was evaluated is a slightly earlier version than that discussed in the previous chapters.

3. Questionnaire: At the end of a session users were given a written questionnaire. This was designed to elicit comments about each different aspect of the system. We were concerned with both their problems with the system and their subjective assessment. The questionnaire was only used in the second stage of the evaluation.

4. Unstructured interview: Users were interviewed at the end of the session, to clarify issues uncovered through observation or through the written questionnaire.

7.1.2 Identifying Problems with the System

Problems with the system could be identified from each of the sources of information discussed above. In this section we will go through the problems identified in the different aspects of the system which we were concerned with evaluating: the use of text and graphics; the explanation content; the dialogue; and the user model.

The Use of Text and Graphics There were two substantial problems with the use of text and graphics. First, users found it hard to switch attention between the graphics and text windows. Almost every utterance has an associated graphical action, but keeping track of what was going on in both windows was not easy. It would be possible to improve things slightly by highlighting graphical actions more clearly. However, the general problem illustrates a fundamental limitation of text-based interaction. Spoken output would allow the user to stay (visually) focused on the diagram, and may prove a more effective mode of communication for multimedia systems.

The second problem concerned the fine coordination of graphical and textual actions. This is done at the sentence level. A graphical action can coincide with any sentence being printed. However, in places some users would have preferred to see graphical actions taking place after the associated noun phrase in the sentence. For example, in a sentence beginning "When the light-dependent resistor has a high input voltage ..." it might be more effective to pause at this point to display and highlight this value before continuing the sentence. This would also correspond better with the use of gestures in human verbal interaction, as described by Kendon [Ken83]. To allow this would require a relatively major change in the system.

Problems with the Content   There were two main types of problem with the content of the explanations. Either information was missing which was required, or inappropriate explanations were given following user questions.

Missing information included information about the role or function of a component in a particular circuit (e.g., "This inverter is needed so that the light goes on when it is cold, not hot"), basic information about wires, voltages, resistance, etc., and any explanation of the behavior of the potential divider circuit. An explanation of the light unit, for example, was always given in terms of a potential divider circuit even when that circuit type was not familiar to the user. This latter problem could be partially fixed by making the behavior of the potential divider an additional prerequisite topic for these explanations. However, the other problems are harder to deal with, requiring changes in the underlying domain models. The role of a component is hard to determine from the underlying circuit model [dK84], while representing this information explicitly in the models, for every component in every circuit, would make the models themselves very complex. Extending the system so that it can explain behavior in terms of more basic electrical concepts would also require major changes in the models. The system assumes that everything is reducible to simple component or circuit behaviors, and it has no knowledge of electrical laws, such as $V = IR$. It is therefore suitable as a tool for learning about simple electronic systems, given knowledge of electricity, but not suitable for real novices.

Inappropriate responses to user questions were partly due to badly phrased question menus. However, the problem also reflects the lack of context dependence in the way questions were interpreted (addressed by Moore [Moo89]). Users should also be able to renegotiate the question topic (e.g., "No, I don't mean that, I mean ...") as observed in the transcripts of human explanations (e.g., utterance 21, second dialogue, appendix A.3).

Problems with the Dialogue   Overall people were happy with the style of interaction, but some felt they had insufficient control. The evaluated version of the system did now allow insertion sequences (where the user asks a question in response to a question) or follow-up questions (at the end of an explanation). These features have since been added. The evaluated version also did now allow users to request the system to repeat or abandon sections of the discourse. Again, this was simply added, using the discourse model as the basis of a menu-based interface allowing the user to reference particular discourse segments.

Another problem occurred when the user asked a number of consecutive questions. The system interpreted these as nested interruptions, and at the end of the sequence it provided repeated resuming or discourse *pop* markers and meta-comments (ie, "Anyway..., Anyway..., Anyway..."). Further work is needed to determine exactly how to resume a discourse given nested or sequential interruptions.

Occasionally, users found the dialogue slightly incoherent and would have preferred more meta-comments explaining what was going on. For example, when explaining the most complex circuit, the focus shifts quite suddenly from discussing the behavior of a circuit section to discussing the function of the overall device. This needs to be marked more clearly. Also, users tended to find it confusing if questions were asked immediately following an interrupting sequence (e.g., "Anyway, what's the output voltage of the light-dependent resistor going to be ..."). We need to consider both whether the use of meta-comments should depend on the level of understanding (or confusion) of the user, and exactly how the presence of an interruption may affect the way an explanation should continue.

Finally, from the scripts it was apparent that the system did not always continue a dialogue appropriately after an interruption (see appendix C.1). In particular, it would sometimes reexplain topics that were explained within an interrupting sequence. This is because the system only "prunes" topics from the explanation plan which directly correspond to the topic of a question asked. However, for subtopics, explained in another context, it may still explain them (depending on the user model). Again, we need a better basis for deciding how the content of a continuing explanation should depend on the content of interrupting sequences.

Problems with the User Model   There were a number of problems with the user model inferences. These were in general too conservative, as the system always decreased its assessment of the user's level of expertise as the session progressed. This would tend to happen more with people who asked a lot of questions of the system. Each time the user asks a question the system adjusts the level of expertise according to

the difficulty of the question. As a consequence, an expert who asked
a large number of questions, then quit the explanation before the system began questioning him, was downgraded to a novice by the end of
the session, while a novice who correctly answered a number of system
questions by guesswork and by examining the past explanation (but who
did not ask many questions) did somewhat better. The EDGE system
supports a range of styles of interaction. Some users tended to ask far
more questions and to play a relatively dominant role in controlling the
interaction, while others followed through the system's explanation, just
asking a few questions at the end. When the user took a more dominant
role the user modeling inferences were particularly unreliable.

Another apparent error with the user modeling system arose with
consecutive questions. The system assumes that the user doesn't know
something if they ask a question about it, but that they maybe know
it if their question is answered and they acknowledge that answer. But
if they ask another question instead of acknowledging the answer, the
system is left thinking they don't know the concept. There is no way
for the user to indicate that they understand the last utterance but that
they want to ask another question, as the user's acknowledgments also
automatically serve the function of indicating that the system should
continue its explanation. This needs to be improved, either by allowing
distinct *acknowledge* and *continue* actions, or by allowing later acknowledgments to serve multiple functions — acknowledging that the last
utterance is understood, and that therefore the utterance before the in-
terruption/repair is also understood. If the latter approach is taken then
Clark and Schaefer's model of nested discourse *contributions* might be
relevant [CS89].

7.1.3   Assessment of the System: The User's Opinion

The questionnaire given to the users at the end of the session gave an
indication of their subjective view of the system. The results suggested
that overall the users found the system acceptable and the dialogues
coherent (apart from problems mentioned above). In general the users
thought that the explanations were at the right level of difficulty, the
meta-comments and discourse markers helpful, and the English, including pronoun use, acceptable. Almost all users thought that asking questions, being asked questions, and having coordinated text and graphics
were all important in an explanation of this sort. A novice who was not

familiar with circuit diagrams rated graphics unimportant, and a relative expert who had a question-asking style of interaction rated being asked questions unimportant. All users enjoyed using the system, to varying degrees.

7.1.4   Conclusion

The evaluation discussed here is very much a preliminary exploration of the system and underlying approach, given a particular domain and a particular class of users. From it we can conclude that the approach at least has potential. People enjoyed using the system and found the basic style of interaction coherent and helpful. It also has a number of problems. Some of these were minor, and relatively easily fixed in later versions. However, some seem to suggest a more radical change in the approach. In particular, the system appeared less effective when the user took a more dominant role in the dialogue. The EDGE framework is appropriate for primarily system-dominated interactions, but where more equal control is appropriate, alternative architectures may need to be considered. This issue is discussed further in the next section.

Further evaluation is required both to evaluate the approach given a more realistic application and operational context, and to explore the tradeoffs and interactions between the different system components. In particular, it would be valuable to explore the contribution of the different system components (i.e., user model, content planning, and dialogue planning) to the effectiveness and acceptability of explanations in different applications.

7.2   Assessment and Further Work

The empirical evaluation discussed above gives an indication of the problems and limitations of this particular implementation. However, it is also important to consider the limitations in the overall architecture and how these may be remedied. In this section we will therefore focus on more theoretical problems, to do with the general approach to text planning, dialogue control, and user modeling.

7.2.1   The Planning Approach

The planning approach used is very simple. Planning rules are used to incrementally expand goals into subgoals, and actions are executed as soon as they are planned. There is no backtracking or search involved, though "failure" indicated by the user can prompt plan repair.

There are inherent restrictions in this approach. It is based on the assumption that there is little interaction between the subgoals — that is, that achieving one subgoal will not destroy the effects of another. Incremental planning does not guarantee an optimal or even a complete solution where there is one, as it is impossible to use later planning decisions to influence earlier ones. As no backtracking is allowed, planning rules must be written in such a way that it is always possible to find a plan to satisfy a given subgoal, and so that later planning decisions will not invalidate earlier ones.

Although the approach is inadequate as a general planning framework for complex problems, it may still be appropriate for our application, as suggested in chapter 1. A dialogue system has to plan in an uncertain world, where assumptions about that world (i.e., the user's knowledge) are continuously being updated. It is more important to be able to react to those changes, and to any problems with the plan, than to be able to generate an "optimal" plan first off. Similar points have been made in the robot planning community, where the world is often changing and unpredictable. *Situated action* is more important than sophisticated planning techniques (e.g., [AC87]). Suchman makes a similar point based on an analysis of human-computer interaction [Suc87]. And existing approaches to text planning (e.g., [Moo89, May91b]) have successfully used similar simple planning approaches.

However, the limitations of the approach led to the following problems. First, because the system does not plan ahead in any detail, it cannot reason about the length and complexity of a forthcoming discourse segment. There is therefore no way of dynamically deciding when to add discourse markers and meta-comments based on this complexity. In practice this meant that a meta-comment or marker might be given to announce that something was about to be explained, yet because of the user's prior knowledge this explanation might consist of a single utterance (or even no utterance at all!).

Second, if you haven't yet determined how to explain something, it is impossible to accurately describe the prerequisite knowledge required as background to that explanation. It is impossible to separate *how* to explain something from exactly *what* is to be included in that explanation. For example, a process may be explained at different levels of detail, with different causal events included in the different explanations. Depending on this level of detail the background information required is quite different. This introduces problems if you want to provide this background information before the process explanation begins. One way round this is to have different rules for explaining a topic, these rules having different preconditions, with the particular rule invoked chosen on the basis of current assumptions about the user's knowledge. With a little effort, the rules can be designed in such a way that the preconditions and eventual explanation strategies chosen should match up. However, assumptions about the user's knowledge might change and another explanation strategy (requiring different background knowledge) might eventually be selected. Determining appropriate background information is a difficult problem, and good solutions may not be possible in the existing simple incremental planning framework.

Third, as the system has only an outline future plan it often does not know whether the user's interrupting question will be addressed later in the discourse. It might be addressable later, but not yet have been added to the plan. There are cases where the system should arguably postpone the user's question, but does not have an adequate representation of the future discourse to decide to do that.

All these problems occur because the system does not know how it will explain something until it has actually begun that explanation. The future "plan" only consists of a few high level goals, not detailed plans. It would be worth exploring whether a limited amount of provisional planning ahead could be used to provide a more extended representation of the future plan, allowing the system to reason further about what it is about to say. This would be possible within the framework described here, with a fairly minor change to the planning algorithm.

7.2.2 Content Planning

As well as the general limitations in the overall planning approach, there are particular problems with the approach to content planning, which is somewhat domain dependent. The approach is based on defining subskill and prerequisite relationships between general types of concept (such as "how something works" or "a device's function"). It can be viewed as a development of schema-based approaches [McK85, Par88], attempting to further *explain* text structure in terms of the relationships between the concepts being explained. However, it has a number of limitations.

First, it fails to capture domain-independent relations between text sections (cf. [MT87a, Hov88, MP89]). In particular, *background, summary/conclusion*, and *sequence* relationships are either not represented or are captured in an ad hoc manner. The solution to this problem is not simply to adopt Moore or Hovy's approach to text planning. We need to be able to use knowledge of how different kinds of concepts can be explained in terms of others, as well as knowledge of general purpose relations. For example, we need to be able to say that a *process* consists of a *sequence* of *causal-events*, and leave it up to the text planner to structure the text and add any appropriate discourse markers based on knowledge of the general sequence relation. While the EDGE system has underemphasized general rhetorical relationships, Moore and Hovy have arguably underemphasized (or left implicit) more domain-related communication knowledge (cf. [KKR91]). A combined approach may be fruitful, though there are significant difficulties to overcome.

Second, it still does not provide a fully adequate basis for deciding what material is optional, only to be included if not already understood. We noted that this decision depended on the role of the material in the text. However, this role cannot be fully specified locally, in a context independent manner, and captured in the prerequisite and subgoal relations in a single planning rule. It is based on higher level discourse relations. For example, individual causal events describing the behavior of a device may each be essential when used as part of a summary or conclusion, following an explanation of the processes involved, but optional when individual component behaviors are described as background information. The current EDGE system cannot make this distinction, where the subgoals of a planning rule should be optional in one context but not in another. This notion of optionality as depending on discourse role needs to be more fully developed, once rhetorical relations are incorporated more explicitly.

Third, the system fails to provide general, "concept-independent" descriptions of alternative explanation strategies such as using analogies. The use of such strategies should be separated more clearly from the representation of subskill and prerequisite relationships, used as the basis for the current planning rules.

Finally, some of the details of the content planning rules are currently specific to the class of device being explained (i.e., electronic systems). We could straightforwardly extend the approach to allow alternative specialized versions of rules for alternative types of objects. For example, the top level *how-it-works* rule might be applicable for all objects, but different versions of the *function* and *process* rules might be available for different types of objects. The planning rules would then be used in conjunction with a device type hierarchy, allowing both general rules and very specific rules for different objects. This would allow the system to be used to effectively explain a wide variety of types of physical device, without writing a whole new set of planning rules for each (significantly) different type of object.

7.2.3   Dialogue Control

The EDGE approach to dialogue planning assumes that the system is dominant and has an overall plan for the discourse. User contributions are treated as interruptions, and the partially planned discourse is always resumed at the end of the interruption. This is a fairly restricted approach to dialogue control, and the system does not respond appropriately when the user takes a more dominant role — it keeps trying to get back to what it was saying before. This raises the question of how to support more equal roles between system and user, and given these more equal roles, how to make the discourse more genuinely adaptive to the user's contributions.

The first step would be to make the dialogue actions that are available to the system and user more symmetric, so that the user could initiate transactions on new topics and inform the system about what they thought was going on. This would be possible in the current framework (given a more complex menu or natural language interface). However, having allowed the user a more dominant role we need to decide how to better respond to their utterances. This might involve interpreting their utterance in context (as Moore does for user questions [Moo89]), inferring their information-seeking plans [Car89], and even developing joint discourse plans [GS90, CL91]. In our case this would be a plan for enabling the user to understand the desired material.

If the user had a more dominant role it might no longer be appropriate to view user utterances as interruptions. The system should reason more dynamically and opportunistically about what to say next. It may be inappropriate to use high level dialogue structures, and to maintain a high level dialogue plan. More local rules may prove more effective, as used by Frohlich and Luff [FL90]. User and system may be viewed as equal agents, cooperating and negotiating in order to learn [Bla90, Bak89, PB89].

7.2.4 User Modeling

The EDGE user modeling component provides a simple way of updating assumptions about the user's knowledge in the context of an explanatory dialogue. It is based on the overlay paradigm, which assumes that the student's knowledge is a subset of the expert's, and does not represent misconceptions. There is an implicit assumption that the system has all relevant knowledge and cannot learn from the user.

Although the model is simple, we suggest that there is more to be gained from the empirical testing and refinement of such simple models than by extending the theoretical framework. There is little concrete evidence as yet concerning the effectiveness of user modeling at improving the acceptability of system explanations. Too little research is concerned with actually evaluating user modeling components, and demonstrating (and improving) their usefulness. Some problems with the EDGE user modeling component, based on our empirical evaluation, were discussed in section 7.1.2.

Having said that, there are a number of directions in which the theoretical framework could be extended, discussed in section 5.2.5. These include extending the range of inferences made on the basis of the user's utterances; extending the range of domain-based inferences, using theories of human plausible inference and learning; and extending the representation of the user model itself, beyond simple overlay modeling, to include misconceptions and/or user goals.

7.2.5 Summary

The EDGE approach has a number of theoretical limitations which suggest directions for further work. The planning approach on the one hand does not provide a fully adequate model of the future discourse, and on the other hand is not fully responsive to a changing context, which might invalidate the future plan entirely. Although the EDGE system provides an effective and practical compromise, further research should explore more powerful and more flexible planning approaches. The content planning rules are somewhat domain specific, and do not capture general purpose rhetorical relations except in an *ad hoc* manner. Further research is needed to combine knowledge of how to explain different types of concept with knowledge of rhetorical relations. The dialogue planning rules are adequate for system-dominated dialogues, but would need extending and adapting to allow dialogues where the user and system had more equal roles. And the user modeling rules need refining based on further empirical evaluation, and could be extended to allow a wider range of user attributes to be represented.

We expect that most of these extensions may be accommodated in the basic EDGE architecture. More sophisticated planning or user modeling techniques could be added without changing other components of the system. The EDGE system therefore provides a basic starting point and framework for the systematic development and evaluation of future explanatory dialogue systems.

7.3   Conclusion: Contributions and Applications

Despite the problems outlined above, the EDGE model provides an effective and practical approach to the problem of generating interactive explanations which depend on assumptions about the user's knowledge. The discourse generated is coherent, as both the content and dialogue planning rules capture coherent discourse structures observed in human explanatory dialogues. It should also be understandable, as the content planning depends heavily on assumptions about the user's knowledge. These assumptions are updated as the explanation progresses; and as the explanation is planned incrementally, changing assumptions about the user's knowledge will influence the detailed planning of the explanation. If there are still difficulties with the explanation, these can be dealt with as they occur, using remediation and repair strategies which provide local responses to particular problems.

The approach integrates ideas from a number of different areas, such as text planning (e.g., [Moo89]), curriculum planning (e.g., [Mur89]), discourse structure (e.g., [GS86, SC75]), and user modeling (e.g., [Chi89, Sle85]). The contribution of the work lies primarily in the way these different ideas are combined to solve a particular important problem — generating interactive explanations.

There are a number of possible applications of this work. First, the approach could be used as a basis for tutorial dialogue systems, allowing a truly mixed initiative dialogue within a complex explanation. In this context, explanation generation is viewed as a microcosm of the whole tutorial process and not relegated to an interface issue (cf. [Wen87, pg 397]). It involves knowledge of tutorial discourse structure, user modeling, and remediation strategies, as well as how to present the underlying knowledge.

Second, it could be used as a basis for computer help systems, providing "interactive manual pages" tailored to the user. Existing work on intelligent help systems has been based on providing short responses to user questions or recognized user need (e.g., [BWS87, Chi89]). However, an explanation of a complex command or system concept may involve a large number of utterances. Allowing interaction within that explanation will improve the usability of the system and the comprehensibility of its explanations.

Third, advisory systems may be based on a similar approach. Jullien and Marty, for example, describe an advisory system which has a provisional plan for finding out information and giving advice on personal finance [JM89]. The system revises and extends this plan, given the user's contributions to the discourse, in a similar manner to the EDGE system. The EDGE system further demonstrates how the information given may depend on the user's knowledge, and how this may be updated in the context of a dialogue.

Finally, explanations given by expert systems may in some cases be complex, requiring a similar type of dialogue. Moore has demonstrated how such explanations can be planned and follow-up questions answered in context [Moo89]. We further demonstrate how interactions with the user may be managed *within* the planned explanation.

Future work should be concerned on the one hand with developing and testing practical applications in order to assess the usefulness of the approach for human-computer interaction, and on the other hand with more theoretical developments, as discussed in the last section. For the former, we need to look for good practical test domains where useful interactive explanation systems may be developed based on the relatively simple approach developed so far. For the latter, we particularly need to consider in more detail how discourse may be managed when each participant (system and user) has their own goals, both individual and shared, with new goals emerging as the dialogue progresses. An explanatory dialogue should be viewed as a particular type of mixed initiative dialogue where the shared overall goal of the participants is for one (or both) participants to understand some potentially complex piece of knowledge. Each participant may have their own beliefs and subgoals concerning how this may be best realized, and the dialogue should include the negotiation and establishment of shared goals.

A Human Circuit Explanations

This appendix will include a selection of complete human explanations of circuit behavior, some with partial suggested analyses of the explanation. It will include a set of five uninterrupted verbal explanations of different types of circuit, two explanations taken from text books, and five explanatory dialogues, illustrating different dialogue styles.

The circuit diagrams used in the explanations are similar to the ones used in the EDGE system, illustrated in appendix B.4.

A.1 Uninterrupted Explanations

The first four of these explanations were given by the same person, who gave comparatively clear explanations.

A.1.1 Light Detector

1. Well, this here looks to be a potential divider circuit
2. and it contains two components
3. one of which is a light-dependent resistor
4. and the other is a variable resistor.
5. The purpose of this circuit is to provide a varying output voltage on this line here.
6. The idea is that when light falls on this light-dependent resistor its resistance changes,
7. so therefore because the resistance of this series circuit has changed the voltage at this point here can change.
8. So, when light falls on the LDR the resistance of this part of the circuit is very low
9. and so this voltage here is a high voltage.
10. In darkness the resistance of the LDR is large
11. and so the voltage at this point drops to a low value.
12. So, we can get a high or low output depending on how much light is falling on the light-dependent resistor.

This example was examined in chapter 2, and the *content* of the utterances classified as:

- *Identification.* "This is a potential divider circuit."
- *Constituency.* "and it contains ..."
- *Function.* "The purpose ..."

- *Process.* Lines 6–11 (consisting of *cause-effect* propositions giving the causal process for different sorts of inputs).
- *Behavior.* "So we can get ..."

Utterance 12 also has a clear *role*, serving as a conclusion or summary.

A.1.2   Heat Detector

1. Well, this is similar to the one above
2. except instead of a light-dependent resistor, we've got a thermistor
3. which is a device whose resistance varies with temperature,
4. so as the temperature rises, then so does the resistance of the thermistor, or is it the other way round. There's a variation in temperature anyway in the thermistor.
5. And so this component will vary with temperature,
6. and so the voltage at this point here will vary also.
7. So, depending on how high or low the temperature is, this will determine whether we have a high of low output at this line here.

This can be classified as starting with a description (*structure*) where the device is *compared* with a similar device, first mentioning the *similarity* (utterance 1), then the *differences* in the *components* (utterances 2–4). A simple *process* description is given in utterances 5–6, followed by a *summary* of *behavior*.

A.1.3   Inverter

1. Well, this is a circuit that has a transistor in it,
2. and assuming that this line here represents an output voltage,
3. its state, that is whether it's high or low, will depend on what voltage we have applied.
4. So, for example, in this case here, if a positive voltage is applied to that input the transistor will conduct,
5. so the voltage at the bottom of that resistor there becomes close to 0.
6. And so a high input provides a low output.
7. Conversely, a low input will provide a high output.
8. So this inverts the voltage.

This example can be broadly classified as: *constituency* (1), *component* (3), *process* (4–5), and a *summary* of *behavior* (6–8).

A.1.4 Low Heat Warning

1. This is a circuit which contains two transistors, and a potential divider setup again.
2. So the idea here with the thermistor is that as the temperature changes the input voltage to the base of the transistor varies also.
3. So it will be either high or low depending on the ambient temperature.
4. Well, let's assume for the moment that the voltage to the base of the transistor goes high.
5. This would mean that the voltage at the collector of transistor T1 is going to be low,
6. which will mean that transistor T2 is not conducting
7. so the lamp will not light.
8. If it is the other way round so that the transistor is shut off, the voltage here is high,
9. which means that the transistor is now going to conduct
10 which means that the lamp will light.

This is an explanation of a slightly more complex circuit. The example may be classified as: *constituency* (1), *component* (2–3), *process* (4–10). The *component* explanation is in fact a description of the behavior of a circuit subsection (the "heat detector unit" section). The *process* section explains behavior at a slightly higher level than the smaller circuits, leaving out steps where they are clear. As in some of the other explanations, the process is split into two sections, going through sequences of events for contrasting input values.

A.1.5 Low Heat Warning

The final example in this section is an explanation of the heat warning circuit by another expert, to illustrate at least some consistency across explainers.

1. This is a circuit with a lamp, and a thermistor.
2. It's got two transistors which look like they are a two stage inverting amplifier.
3. So as the temperature of the thermistor varies the brightness of the bulb will vary as well.
4. There's also the potentiometer so the range of brightness can effectively be varied as well.

5. So, as the temperature goes up I think the resistance goes down on the thermistor.

6. Which means that transistor T1 will be turned on more

7. and the voltage at the collector of T2 will go down

8. and this will turn off T2

9. and make the bulb go dimmer.

10. So it looks like the light will come on when it gets cold.

This begins with a relatively complex *constituency* description (1–2), (arguably) a description of the *function* of the circuit (3) and of a particular *component* (4) (though this could also be classified as *behavior*), followed by a *process* description (5–9) and *summary* of *behavior* (10).

These five examples illustrate common patterns of description across a range of circuits and two experts. There are of course many examples which are less coherent, often involving just a hesitant process sequence. But the ones chosen above capture much of the richness of this sort of explanation, where the expert has a good understanding of the domain.

A.2   Textbook Explanations

Textbook explanations of the same circuits are very similar to the clearer verbal explanations, but depend more on the context of the explanation in the textbook — the artificial setting of the verbal explanations effectively eliminated this context. They may include additional information, for example, explaining why this explanation is being given at this point in the textbook. They may also leave out information introduced in a previous section. For example, the two circuits below had already been identified in the preceding section of the textbook as potential divider circuits with output voltage depending on input heat/light intensity. The following two examples are taken from [Joh87] and follow a discussion of potential divider circuits:

A.2.1   Light Detector

"This is a basic circuit consisting of a transducer and a resistor as described in the previous section (Figure 4.15). The transducer is an LDR (section 3.3) and it forms the upper half of the potential divider. If the intensity of the light falling upon the LDR increases, the resistance of the LDR will fall. The output voltage from the potential divider will therefore rise.

"The potential divider will give the greatest change in output voltage when the resistances of the LDR and lower resistor are equal, and the resistor is made variable so that this can be achieved. By adjusting the potentiometer it is possible to operate the circuit successfully over a wide range of light intensities."

A.2.2 Heat Detector

"Once again a potential divider is used with a transducer as the upper resistor, but this time the transducer is a thermistor (section 3.2). As the temperature of the thermistor rises so too does the output voltage of the circuit (See figure 4.16). The resistor is a potentiometer connected as a variable resistor to allow for different temperature ranges.

"In spite of the similarities in their circuits, the light unit and the heat unit are very different to use as parts of a system. The resistance of an LDR varies from nearly infinity in the dark to a few hundred ohms in a good light. When the LDR resistance is infinite, the output voltage will be close to zero, and when it is at its lowest the voltage will approach Vcc. This very large range in output voltages makes light operated systems easy to design.

"The resistance of a thermistor falls by no more than a factor of ten, which produces an output voltage change of only a few volts. This makes the design of the next stage in the system much more crucial."

Note that even these written explanations are, in a sense, interactive. The reader is referred to diagrams and other sections of the book, which they can turn to if required.

A.3 Dialogues

This section includes a number of examples of complete dialogues with novices about circuit behavior. They are chosen to illustrate a range of interactional styles. Fragments of these explanations were discussed in chapter 2. The first two examples are with more or less complete novices, resulting in largely unstructured dialogues dominated by the novice's questions. All the dialogues are by different subjects (expert and novice).

A.3.1   Novice-Dominant-Informing Dialogue: Light Detector

The first example was introduced in figure 2.17. It illustrates a dialogue
which is dominated by follow-up questions, following a very short but
coherent explanation from the expert who misjudges the novice's knowledge. In this extreme example, many of the follow-up answers are never
completely given, but are interrupted by more basic questions. The
example illustrates the problems and confusions which may arise in a
simple explanatory dialogue when the novice does not have the requisite
knowledge. It therefore indicates the usefulness of at least having some
model of what the user knows, learned from the interaction or direct
questions.

E: 1. In this circuit we have an output whose voltage depends on the amount
   of light falling on the LDR

   2. and the more light falls on here the more it will conduct

   3. so the higher the voltage will be here.

N: 4. What does LDR stand for?

E: 5. Light-dependent resistor.

N: 6. What's this bit?

E: 7. That bit's a variable resistor so you can change how the output level
   varies with the resistance of the LDR.

N: 8. Say that again..

E: 9. Well, this is a potential divider here, so the potential here will be between 0 and 9V in proportion to the resistance of these two things.

N: 10. What's potential?

E: 11. The voltage.

N: 12. Why do you call it potential?

E: 13. Because that's what trendy people call it.

N: 14. and this is a variable resistance?

E: 15. Yes, that's right.

N: 16. Why does it say 5K on it?

E: 17. Because its maximum resistance is 5,000 Ohms.

N: 18. Right. Does it matter where these things are?

E: 19. Yes, if you switch them round it will work the other way round, and
   the voltage will go down as the light increases.

N: 20. Why?

E: 21. Because, the ratio, the output will vary between 0 and 9V in proportion
   to the ratio of the two resistances,

22. so the bigger the resistance here, the further it will be away from 0V.

N: 23. Is there any way you can find out what the resistance is in that, at any given point?

E: 24. Well, if you know what the resistance of this is, you know what the output voltage is

25. then you know that the ratio of the resistance of the light-dependent resistor to the variable resistor here is the same as the ratio of the voltage difference between 9V and the output and the output and 0V.

N: 26. The output comes out here? What comes out here?

E: 27. That's where your 9V goes in, you connect these to your battery.

N: 28. I see, that's why it says plus there..

E: 29. This is at 0V and this is at plus 9V. It says plus because it's a positive voltage. It could be −9V.

N: 30. So what's happening here?

E: 31. You could just choose an arbitrary.. voltages are relative things, you can choose an arbitrary voltage as your 0V point.

N: 32. Why is there a different voltage in different places?

E: 33 Because there's a battery attached to it, which they don't show. So when they do this they really mean there's a battery here. *(draws battery)*. It's a 9V battery.

N: 34. And this is the positive pole and this is the..

E: 35. Just so, so this one is 9V higher than this one. We could cross this out and say −300V here and this would be −291V. All you've got is the difference between them is 9V.

N: Alright.

E: Enough of that one.

A.3.2   Expert-Dominant-Informing Dialogue: Light Detector

The next example (introduced in figure 2.16) illustrates a case where the expert dominates the interaction, and apparently attempts to get back to their original planned explanation after novice interruptions. In this case the explanation is given in terms of circuit equations rather than inputs and outputs, but the same pattern of explanations applies. This example will be marked according to the author's perception of where interruptions begin and end, marking interrupting sequences with the symbol ◇. The example also illustrates the importance of the novice's signals indicating when they understand.

E: 1. These components here, you might consider them as being both resistors. Two variable resistors. I can write down a relation for resistance..

N: 2. ◇ You'll have to tell me what a resistor is.

E: 3. ◇ A resistor is an element which if you apply a voltage across it there is a certain current flowing through the resistor. There is a relationship $V = I \times R$..

N: 4. ◇ It doesn't help. What does it do? Does it stop the current getting through?

E: 5. ◇ Yes. If the resistance was nil it would just be a connection here, then the current is mainly restricted by the amount of current.. voltage..

N: 6. ◇ Right, so the resistor has to be, can be of various strengths presumably. And the current going through it has to be of certain strengths before it can get through the resistor?

E: 7. ◇ No, in this case the current is determined by the strength of your power supply and you can rewrite this relation to $I = V \div R$, where if this is constant, say 10V or 9V battery for example, changing this resistor changes the current through the resistor. If this one becomes nil you get an infinite current. If it's high then the current becomes low.

N: 8. ◇ I see, or at least I think I see.

E: 9. Well, this circuit here are just two resistors, switched in serial mode. You can think of it as one resistor supplied with a voltage 9V, and there will be a current flowing through the circuit.

10. Well, the output can be calculated by, when you know the current flowing through here then you assume that the output voltage is determined by the current multiplied by this resistance. In order to calculate the current you have to include this resistor in your network as well..

N: 11. ◇ Why are we bothered about what the current is through there then? What's going to happen? I have to know the purpose of it.

E: 12. ◇ In the end you want to know this voltage. The output voltage here relates to the input voltage, and your current can be assumed as constant, not as constant, as variable depending on the value of the resistance.

N: 13. ◇ OK.

E: 14. I can just write down a relationship, this is I1, the output voltage is I1/ (*writes equation*).

N: 15. Right.

E: 16. Light on the resistor — this is a light sensitive resistor — changes this value, your resistance value of this element changes, so in the end your output voltage changes as well.

N: 17. ◇ Why would that change naturally, in daylight?

–: 18. *clarification from experimenter*

N: 19. ⋄ A sudden change in light will change that, so what happens? This is a very kind of low level description, and without knowing why it's worthwhile having your voltage be anything, I mean, why don't you just plug it into the mains?

E: 20. ⋄ Maybe I better explain it on a higher level.

N: 21. ⋄ I mean, what is the point of this particular bit, that is really what I want to know, rather than an explanation at a lower level.

E: 22. ⋄ OK, well, you want to have varying output signal depending on the light falling on this input here, and you also want to set the sensitivity of this element as well, and that's done by this varying resistor. The amount of light, there is a direct relationship between the change in voltage here and the light falling on there, but the level on which your voltage changes can be adjusted by this resistor. So it will change maybe ten percent at 5V, when this one is set, depending on the light falling, or you can adjust the threshold a little bit so it's 6V or 7V.

N: 23. ⋄ So you can make it more or less sensitive, I mean, this one must be sensitive to what the LDR is doing?

E: 24. ⋄ I think sensitivity is a property of the LDR itself.

N: 25. ⋄ OK.

E: 26. Is that sufficient?

N: 27. I think I know what's going on with it, with the first bit.

This example isn't a particularly clear explanation. It follows the basic *components, process* description in utterances 1, 9–10 and 16, but confuses the novice with unnecessary details. However, it is a rich source of examples of how interruptions are managed. The end of an interruption is signaled by the novice with "OK" or "I see", and then the expert apparently continues the main explanation, in one case repeating part of the previous explanation.

The novice gives some acknowledgment that she understands in a number of places, indicating that she has followed the last utterance (utterance 15), that she accepts the answer to a question (utterances 8, 13, and 25) and when she has understood the circuit (utterance 27). These acknowledgments are vital if the expert is to recognize problems and adjust the level of and quantity of explanation appropriately.

A.3.3   Expert-Dominant-Tutorial Dialogue: Inverter

This example shows a dialogue where the expert dominates, but involves the novice by asking directed questions. An extract was given in figure 2.19.

E: 1. OK, do you remember anything about transistors?

2. Basically, the important thing about transistors is, you've got three ends to it, the middle one, that's called the base, and current going through the other two, and also a little bit going through the base. And typically you get a little current going through the base and a big current going through the other two, and the current you get going through the base controls the current through the other two.

3. In other words, you can think of it as a varying resistor between the two, which, when there's a lot of current going through here, the resistance is low so a lot of current goes through these two. And when there's no current going through the base, there's no current going through these two

4. and it acts as an amplifier, so the current going through the collector and emitter

N: 5. is amplified?

E: 6. is 100 or 200 times bigger than the current going through here.

7. The arrow here just tells you which way round you should connect it.

8. Right, so what's going to happen here, say, if you consider this as an input and this as an output, what happens when you make this voltage high, what happens to this?

N: 9. When you make it high you probably get all the current from this end amplified.

E: 10. Well, when you make the current high..

N: 11. It opens the gate.

E: 12. What's going to happen to the resistance between here and here?

N: 13. It's going to be low.

E: 14. So, what's going to happen to the voltage here. If you have a very low resistance?

N: 15. It's going to tend to the high limit.

E: 16. Careful, if you let the current through these two, then it's just as if you wired these two up, a little bit, so it's just as if the transistor weren't there and these two are connected.

17. So, if these two are connected there's nothing here in fact. What's the voltage here going to be?

N: 18. Well, the same voltage as the other end.

E: 19. Yes, so it's going to be low.

20. So, when this is high this is low

21. and on the other hand, when the voltage here is low, there will be no current going through here, so what will the voltage be?

N: 22. High.

E: 23. Yes, high, 9V.

This explanation starts with a description of the most complex *component* (1–7). This is followed by a detailed *process* description (8–19) with a *summary* of this *behavior* in utterance 20. Lines 21–23 conclude with a *process* description for a contrasting input value.

The more interesting issues in this explanation relate to the interactions with the novice. The novice is being asked to fill in some of the steps in the explanation — but the content of these steps follows the normal pattern of such explanations. When the novice gets questions wrong there are various strategies adopted for correcting the user — this expert never immediately told the novice the correct answer following an error. Utterances 10–19 illustrate a complex remedial sequence, where each incorrect or partially correct answer leads to further information and further questioning, leading the novice to the correct answer. Utterances 16–17 illustrate a basic strategy used in the EDGE system — if the answer is incorrect, give the user some more information from which they should be able to deduce the answer and ask it again.

A.3.4   Novice-Dominant-Tutorial Dialogue: Heat Detector

This example shows how an explanation may be dominated by the novice, with the expert commenting. An extract was given in figure 2.18. Utterances 1–4 and 7–10 illustrate how an explanation is resumed after an interruption. In the second case it was an interruption from the expert after an incorrect statement from the novice. Again, interrupting subdialogues will be marked with the symbol ◇.

E: 1. Right, the next thing is exactly analogous really..

N: 2. ◇ OK, what's this?

E: 3. ◇ That means it's a variable resistor, it's a resistance that you can vary by turning that little knob, effectively, and it varies from 5,000 Ohms, that's a fairly high resistance, to presumably nothing.

4. Right, the heat detector is exactly analogous in fact.

5. How do you think it works?

N: 6. Right, presumably depending on the amount of heat here, if it has, the more heat it has the more resistance it has?

E: 7. ◇ Probably the less.

N: 8. ◇ The less heat it has the more resistance it has?

E: 9. ◇ Sorry, no, the hotter it is the less resistance.

N: 10. OK, the hotter it is the less resistance.

11. So, if it's not hot at all, if it's cold, if it's very high resistance there-
    fore this middle one is closer to 0, and if it's very very hot it has low
    resistance so it's closer to 9V here.

12. ⋄ But I don't see what difference this 5K or 10K makes?

E: 13. ⋄ It's probably because a thermistor has a high intrinsic, if the relative
    resistances mean that, decide whether it's going to be closer to 9 or 0,
    if this one's low relative to that one then it's closer to 0 and if this one's
    low relative to that one it's 9. And presumably it's variable to allow
    you to tweak it slightly so you can adjust the point at which it swings
    from 9 to 0 exactly.

N: 14. OK.

A.3.5 Cooperative-Informing Dialogue: Burglar Alarm

This final example shows how a complex circuit is explained jointly by
expert and novice. An extract was given in figure 2.20. The dialogue
starts off with the expert assuming a relatively dominant tutorial role,
but soon the roles change and the two participants work out and explain
the circuit behavior together.

E: 1. What I'm going to do is to get you to explain this last circuit to me.
    Before I do that I better say briefly what a comparator is.

2. What this does is compare the inputs and if there's difference it should
   be switched on, if there's no difference it won't be switched on. I think
   it's that way round.

3. I'll tell you what we want from this burglar alarm and you'll try and
   explain how it can be done.

4. Now, we've got a speaker and what we want that to do is when a light
   gets shined on there we want that to go dee dah dee dah. Like that.

5. Now, you know what an astable circuit does. You know how the voltage
   can vary across here, you know that this compares voltages, comparing
   the voltage across there to the voltage coming in there. And we've
   got these two things which are — Can you remember what that circuit
   represents?

N: 6. It's called a NAND.

E: 7. Right, and you know that that's an inverter as well.

N: 8. So, when that goes, when it's off, that shouldn't be working, so I assume
   it's all happy at the moment, so that's at 9, that's at 0.

E: 9. So when there's no light that will tell you that — what resistance, low
   or high?

N: 10. When there's no light that will be low.

E: 11. High, high resistance.

N: 12. Didn't you say that when you shone light on it it got higher?

E: 13. It gets lower.

N: 14. OK, so it's high, so this is 0, so that's 0 and that's 9 so that won't be on 'cause that's at 0.

E: 15. If I've got it right, that will be off, if either are 0 that's going to be a 1, so that's 0.

N: 16. You don't need to worry about this side of the circuit, it's just producing a block wave making the nee naw nee naw sound. So that's 0 then this is off, which means that that's on, this is going on-off all the time, and so that would go nee naw nee naw.

E: 17. Hold on. That's off, that's off, so the potential is at 9V, so that's at 9V, and going ee aw ee aw. Hold on..

N: 18. This should be 1, so that's 1, so that's off, yeah, the transistor is on, but it breaks the circuit, so this is all at 9V.

E: 19. We're talking about a point up here. If that's a NAND, if either of these are off then that point is at 9 up there.

N: 20. Hang on, when we say off do we mean that..

E: 21. Hold on, that's on, that's not what we wanted.

N: 22. Should it be 0?

−: 23. *Clarification from experimenter*

N: 24. So, the circuit should now be on because the light beam has been broken. Let's go through it. This is 1, it doesn't really matter what one is, this will be open, 1, so that will be at 9V. Each time this flicks on or off this will flick on or off and that would go dddddd. If you actually had light on there then..

E: 25. That's not true, this will be switching on or off. What we want is this to be switched off if either of these two is off, and that is always going to be at 9. It doesn't matter whether that's changing or not, that can be 0 or 1, so we actually want that to be 0. If that's a high voltage we get an inverter and that will be switched on.

−: 26. *clarification*

N: 27. It would be an inverter if there was a wire coming out here.

E: 28. Oh, right, but we'll have, that would be raised to 0V.

N: 29. Right, if there's light shining on this, the resistance goes down, which means that this will get to 9, and that's already at 9, so this will be 0, that will be 0, and because we have a 0 here, this is..

E: 30. Up there, that thing there.

N: 31. We have a 0 on the first one.

E: 32. Well, the first one will be going from 0 to 1 all the time.

N: 33. So, looking at the table, that point there, for this whole inverter will be going 1 1, so it will always be on..

—: 34. *clarification*

N: 35. So we've got 1, so this is always going to be 9, so there's always voltage across there.

E: 36. So it's not going to produce a sound. So this is 1, where if you break the light is will..

N: 37. So that's going to happen in that case, and if it's the other case, where there's no light shining on here, this will be 0, this will be at 1, that'll be at 1, so if we draw the table again, that's at 0 and 1 because that will be going up and down, this will be at 0 and this one will be at 1, so this will be varying between 9 and 0 so will be going nee naw nee naw.

Note the use of opening meta-comments in utterances 1 and 3. Also, the circuit concerned consisted of a number of simpler circuits, most of which had been already explained earlier in the session. The one that had not been already explained (the comparator) is introduced explicitly in this explanation (utterance 2). This suggests that modeling the user is of some use. The explanation starts off with this *component* description, then the *function* (line 4), further *components* or circuit sections (4–8) and then *process* (line 9 onward). Much of the explanation consists of repeated attempts by each subject (novice and expert) to get the process sequence right, with occasional clarifications from the experimenter when both parties were confused.

B Planning Rules and Domain Knowledge

In this appendix we include a subset of the planning rules and domain models used in the EDGE system. These are used, together with the discourse planner, user modeling components, and a realization component for linguistic and graphical acts, to generate the simpler example dialogues in the book (e.g., in chapter 1).

B.1 Content Planning Rules

The following content planning rules are the basic rules used to obtain explanations of the simpler circuits. The full system includes a small number of additional rules for obtaining descriptions at different levels of detail. The rules include illustrative information about the difficulty levels of associated concepts.

```
(defplan how-it-works (device)
    :constraints ((device-structure device))
    :preconditions ((know-user structure (device)))
    :subgoals ((d-goal sub.transaction
                    ((c-goal process (device)) 'open))
               (d-goal sub.transaction
                    ((c-goal behavior (device)) 'summary)))
    :template ("how" (ref device) "works")
    :difficulty (((light-unit0) 3)))

(defplan structure (device)
    :constraints ((device-type device))
    :preconditions ((know-user identity (device))
                    (know-user components (device))
                    (know-user function (device)))
    :template ("what" (ref device) "is like")
    :difficulty (((light-unit0) 3)))

(defplan structure (device)
    :constraints ((device-analogy device)
                  (know-user 'structure
                        (list (device-analogy device)) nil))
    :subgoals ((c-goal compare-structure
                    (device (device-analogy device))))
    :template ("what" (ref device) "is like"))
```

```
(defplan identity (device)
   :subgoals ((d-goal teaching.exchange
                 ((list 'kind-of device (device-type device)))))
   :template ("what kind of device" (ref device) "is")
   :difficulty (((light-unit0) 2)))

(defplan compare-structure (device other-device)
   :subgoals ((d-goal teaching.exchange
                 ((list 'similar 'structure device other-device)))
              (c-goal constrast-components (device other-device))
              (c-goal contrast-functions (device other-device)))
   :template ("how" (ref device) "compares with" (ref other-device)))

(defplan compare-function (device other-device)
  :subgoals ((d-goal teaching.exchange
    ((list 'similar 'structure device other-device)))
     (c-goal contrast-functions (device other-device)))
  :template ("how" (ref device) "compares with" (ref other-device)))

(defplan contrast-components (device other-device)
   :subgoals ((d-goal teaching.exchange
                 ((list 'comp-differences
                        (component-differences device
                                               other-device)))))
   :template ("the differences between the components of the"
              (ref device) "and" (ref other-device)))

(defplan constrast-functions (device other-device)
   :subgoals ((d-goal teaching.exchange
                 ((list 'function-differences
                        (first (device-input-values device))
                        (first (device-input-values other-device))
                        (device-output-type device)))))
   :template ("the differences between the function of the" (ref device)
              "and" (ref other-device)))

(defplan function (device)
   :subgoals ((d-goal teaching.exchange
                 ((list 'function device
                        (device-input-values device)
                        (device-output-type device)))))
   :template ("what" (ref device) "is for")
   :difficulty (((light-unit0) 2)))
```

```
(defplan  components (device)
   :constraints ((device-components device))
   :preconditions ((know-user constituency (device))
                   (forall (comp (device-components device))
                           (know-user component (comp))))
   :template ("what" (possref device) "components do"))

(defplan constituency (device)
   :subgoals ((d-goal teaching.exchange
                  ((list 'components-of device)))
              (forall (component (device-components device))
                      (d-goal teaching.exchange
                          ((list 'list-item component)))))
   :template ("what" (possref device) "components are"))

(defplan component (comp)
   :preconditions ((know-user identify-diagram (comp))
                   (know-user behavior (comp)))
   :template ("what" (ref comp) "does"))

(defplan identify-diagram (comp)
  :subgoals ((call point-at (comp))
             (d-goal teaching.exchange
                 ((list 'identify-wrt-diagram comp))))
   :template ("what" (ref device) "looks like."))


(defplan behavior (device)
   :preconditions ((forall (inputs (device-input-values device))
                        (know-user causal-event
                                    (device
                                     inputs
                                     (get-output device inputs)))))
   :template ("what" (ref device) "does")
   :difficulty (((fixed-resistor0) 1)))

(defplan process (device)
   :constraints ((device-structure device))
   :subgoals ((forall (inputs (device-input-values device))
                   (c-goal causal-sequence (device inputs))))
   :template ("how" (ref device) "works given different inputs"))
```

```
defplan causal-sequence (device inputs)
  :subgoals ((d-goal teaching.exchange
                       ((list 'initial-state device inputs)))
             (call display-value ((first inputs)
                                    (first
                                      (device-input-meters device))))
             (c-goal event-sequence (device inputs)))
  :template ("how" (ref device) "works given the following inputs:"
             inputs))

(defplan event-sequence (device inputs)
   :subgoals ((forall (event (deduce-events device inputs))
                      (c-goal causal-event
                              ((event-device event)
                               (event-inputs event)
                               (event-output event)))))
   :template ("how" (ref device)
              "functions when it has the following inputs:"
              inputs))

(defplan causal-event (device inputs output)
   :subgoals ((call display-value ((first inputs)
                      (first (device-input-meters device))))
              (call display-value ((second inputs)
                      (second (device-input-meters device))))
              (d-goal teaching.exchange
                      ((list 'causal-event device inputs output)))
              (call display-value (output
                                     (device-output-meter device))))
   :template ("what the output of" (ref device)
              "is when its inputs are:" inputs)
   :difficulty (((fixed-resistor0 nil '(resistance medium)) 1)))
```

B.2 Discourse Planning Rules

The following plans are used to control interactions with the user and
decisions about the use of meta-comments and discourse markers. The
plans are loosely based on the hierarchical discourse models of Sinclair
and Coulthard and followers. Transaction definitions control the organization of a set of exchanges, such as a single topic or an interrupting
section. Exchange definitions control more detailed interaction with the
user. Move definitions control the sequencing of types of speech act

within a turn. Only the most important rules are included, allowing dialogues such as the one in the first chapter.

B.2.1   Transactions

```
(defplan informing.transaction (goal)
   :subgoals ((d-goal boundary.exchange (goal 'open))
              (d-goal teaching.exchanges (goal))
              (d-goal boundary.exchange (goal 'close))))

(defplan interrupting.transaction (goal oldgoal)
   :subgoals ((d-goal boundary.exchange (goal 'push))
              (d-goal teaching.exchanges (goal))
              (d-goal boundary.exchange (oldgoal 'pop))))

(defplan sub.transaction (goal type)
   :subgoals ((d-goal boundary.exchange (goal type))
              (d-goal teaching.exchanges (goal))
              (d-goal boundary.exchange (goal 'close-sub))))
```

B.2.2   Exchanges

These are the basic exchange definitions. Further exchange types are defined to allow the system to deal with repair requests (where the user indicates they don't understand).

```
(defplan teaching.exchanges (goal)
   :subgoals ((call plan-content (goal))))

(defplan boundary.exchange (goal type)
   :constraints ((member type '(open pop))
                 (role-determines-topic-decisions *system-role*))
   :subgoals ((d-goal framing.move (type))
              (d-goal focusing.move (goal type))))

(defplan boundary.exchange (goal type)
   :constraints ((member type '(summary push open-sub)))
   :subgoals ((d-goal framing.move (type))))    ; only need marker

(defplan boundary.exchange (goal type)
   :constraints ((eql type 'close-sub)
                 (role-pause-every-utterance *system-role*))
   :subgoals ((call null-act)))
```

```
(defplan boundary.exchange (goal type)
   :constraints ((eql type 'close))
   :subgoals ((d-goal suggest-close.move (goal))
              (d-goal pupil-acknowledge.move (goal))))

(defplan teaching.exchange (fact)
   :constraints ((role-system-questions *system-role*)
                 (maybe-understood (goal-parent *activegoal*) nil)
                 (fact-question-template fact))
   :subgoals ((d-goal teacher-elicit.exchange (fact))))

(defplan teaching.exchange (fact)
   :subgoals ((d-goal teacher-inform.exchange (fact))))

(defplan teacher-inform.exchange (fact)
   :constraints ((role-pause-each-utterance *system-role*))
   :subgoals ((d-goal teacher-inform.move (fact))
              (d-goal pupil-acknowledge.move (fact))))

(defplan teacher-elicit.exchange (fact)
   :subgoals ((d-goal teacher-elicit.move (fact))
              (d-goal pupil-reply.move (fact))
              (d-goal teacher-response.move (fact))))
```

B.2.3   Moves and Acts

Note: Only complex moves and acts will be included. Other moves consist of single acts of same name, which in turn consist of single actions.

```
(defplan framing.move (type)
   :subgoals ((d-goal marker.act (type))))

(defplan focusing.move (goal type)
   :subgoals ((d-goal meta-comment.act (goal type))))

;; Teacher reply goal is explicitly placed on agenda when user asks
;; questions when system is pausing.

(defplan teacher-reply.move (question-goal old-goal)
   :constraints ((not (answered-later question-goal)))
   :subgoals ((d-goal interrupting.transaction
                      (question-goal old-goal))))

;; The variable *answer* is set in the pupil-answer move/act.
```

```
(defplan teacher-response.move (fact)
   :subgoals ((d-goal teacher-assess.act (fact *answer*))
              (d-goal teacher-evaluate.act (fact *answer*))
              (d-goal teacher-comment.act (fact *answer*))))

;; The comment act may cause remediation, if such exists.

(defplan teacher-comment.act (fact answer)
   :constraints ((response fact answer))
   :subgoals ((d-goal interrupting.transaction
                      ((response fact answer)
                 *current-goal*))))

(defplan teacher-comment.act (fact answer)
 :subgoals ((call teacher-comment-act (fact answer))))
```

B.3   Remediation Planning Rules

A single illustrative remediation plan is included below:

```
(defplan event-reply (device inputs output)
   :constraints ((device-analogy device)
                 (know-user 'function
                            (list (device-analogy device))
                            nil ))   ;flag to avoid asking user this
   :subgoals ((c-goal compare-function
                      (device (device-analogy device)))
              (d-goal marker.act ('summary))
              (d-goal teacher-elicit.exchange
                 ((list 'causal-event device inputs output)))))
```

B.4   Device Models

The following device definitions allow exploration of the basic system. In the complete system the device instances (e.g., ldr0) would be generated while creating the circuit diagram, and associated input and output meters created and positions recorded so that graphical actions are possible.

Each device has a name, class, typical input values, a function for calculating the device's output given some input(s), possibly some components and structure, a type of output (e.g., voltage), possibly an anal-

ogous device, and some graphics information. Devices inherit properties
from "included" devices.

```
(defstruct (device (:print-function print-device))
  name type input-values output-function components structure
  output-type analogy input-meters output-meter position)

(defstruct (resistor (:include device))
  (name "resistor")
  (type "component")
  (output-type 'resistance))

(defstruct (fixed-resistor (:include resistor))
  (name "fixed resistor")
  (type "resistor")
  (output-type 'resistance)
  (input-values '(nil))
  (output-function (function (lambda nil '(resistance medium)))))

(defstruct (ldr (:include resistor))
  (name "light dependent resistor")
  (type "resistor")
  (input-values '(((light-intensity high))
                  ((light-intensity low))))
  (output-function (function ldr-output)))

(defstruct (thermistor (:include resistor))
  (name "thermistor")
  (type "resistor")
  (input-values '(((heat-intensity high))
                  ((heat-intensity low))))
  (output-function (function thermistor-output)))

(defstruct (pd (:include device))
  (name "potential divider circuit")
  (type "device")
  (output-type 'voltage)
  (input-values  '(((resistance low) (resistance high))
                   ((resistance high) (resistance low))))
  (output-function (function pd-output)))
```

```
(defstruct (heat-unit (:include pd))
  (name "heat detector unit")
  (type "potential divider circuit")
  (input-values '(((heat-intensity high))
((heat-intensity low))))
  (output-function (function heat-unit-output))
  (structure '(lambda (heat)
                 (pd0 (thermistor0 heat) (fixed-resistor0)))))

(defstruct (light-unit (:include pd))
  (name "light detector unit")
  (type "potential divider circuit")
  (input-values '(((light-intensity high))
((light-intensity low))))
  (output-function (function light-unit-output))
  (structure '(lambda (light)
                 (pd0 (ldr0 light) (fixed-resistor0)))))


(defstruct heat-warning (:include device)
  (name "low heat warning circuit")
  (type "warning device")
  (input-values '(((heat-intensity low)) ((heat-intensity high))))
  (output-function (function heat-warning-output))
  (structure '(lambda (heat)
                 (lamp0 (inverter0 (comparator0  (heat-unit0 heat)))))))))


; example test instances and relations

(setf ldr0 (make-ldr)
      thermistor0 (make-thermistor)
      fixed-resistor0 (make-fixed-resistor)
      light-unit0 (make-light-unit))

(setf (device-analogy ldr0) thermistor0
      (device-components light-unit0) (list ldr0 fixed-resistor0))
```

B.5   Circuit Diagrams

The circuit diagrams of the devices explained in the text (chapter 6) are
given below:

Low Heat Warning Circuit

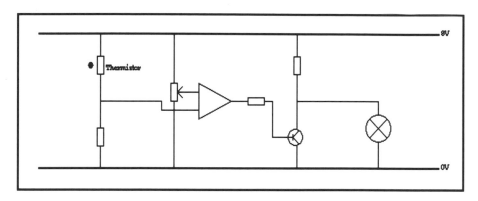

Light Detector Unit

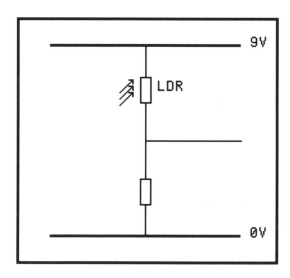

Heat Detector Unit

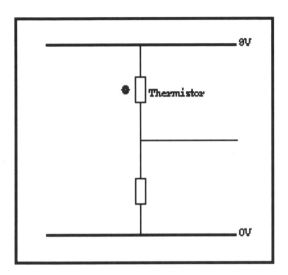

Inverter

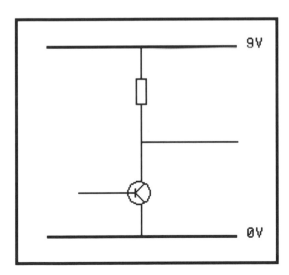

C Example Dialogues with Real Users

The following extracts are taken from the scripts of people using the system, and illustrate its problems as well as its features. Note that the details of the dialogues may not follow the examples in the main text, as based on an earlier version of the system. As before, the system pauses after each numbered utterance.

C.1 User P: Managing Mixed Initiative Interaction

This first example illustrates some of the problems when the user's questions and the system's explanation plan overlap. Should it still say what it was going to say? What criteria can be used to modify and revise plans based on questions already answered?

S: 1. OK, we're going to be explaining how the heat detector works.
Do you know what the heat detector circuit is like?

U: 2. No.

S: 3. A heat detector circuit is a sort of potential divider circuit.

U: 4. What does a heat detector circuit do?

S: 5. I'll be getting on to that in a minute.

U: 6. Do you know what the potential divider circuit does for different inputs?

U: 7. No.

S: 8. Oh well, let's go through what the potential divider circuit does.
When it has one low (fully conducting) input resistance (near 9V rail) and one high (not conducting) input resistance (near 0V rail) then the output voltage (in the middle) is high (9V).

9. When it has one high (not conducting) input resistance (near 9V rail) and one low (not conducting) input resistance (near 0V rail) then the output voltage (in the middle) is high (9V).

10. The heat detector's purpose is to provide an output voltage which depends on the input heat intensity.

11. This component here is a thermistor.

U: 12. How does the thermistor work?

S: 13. Well, a thermistor is a bit complicated to explain in detail so I'll just tell you what it does.

14. When the input heat intensity (H1) of the thermistor is high (hot) the output resistance (R1) will be quite low.

15. When it is low (cold) the output resistance (R1) will be quite high.

16. Anyway, we were in the middle of describing the component: thermistor.

17. Let's go through what the thermistor does.
    What's the output resistance (R1) of the thermistor going to be when
    the input heat intensity is high (hot)?

U: 18. Quite low.

S: 19. Yes, splendid, it's quite low.
    What's it going to be when the input heat intensity is low (cold)?

U: 20. Quite high.

S: 21. Yes, great, it's quite high.
    Now, we're going to be explaining the behavior of the heat detector
    circuit [...]

In this example the answer to a question is deferred because it is already
in the plan (utterance 5) — yet maybe the student knows better than the
system when a particular bit of knowledge should be explained. Later
versions of the system checked with the user whether answers could be
deferred. In line 17 and following, the system essentially explains the
thermistor's behavior a second time, having already described it while
answering the user's question. While the system will avoid reexplaining
a goal which was directly asked by the user, it will reexplain subgoals.
This is clearly not always appropriate.

C.2   User M: Followup Questions and Remediation

The next example illustrates one way that the system responds to incorrect answers to questions, and how questions may be asked at the
end of an explanation. In this session the heat warning circuit is being
explained. The explanation has progressed by the system explaining the
behavior of the circuit at a highest level of detail (in terms of circuit
sections) and asking the user questions. When the user fails to answer
correctly the system shifts down a level, explaining at a lower level of
detail so the user can follow through why the answer was incorrect. The
conclusion of the explanation is given below.

S: 1. What's the output voltage (V7) of the inverter going to be when the
    input voltage (V5) is low (0V)?

U: 2. Quite high (towards 9V).

S: 3. Nope, you lose,
    OK, maybe we better go through what the inverter does when it has a
    low input voltage.
    Suppose the input voltage is low (0V).

4. When the input voltage (V5) of the transistor is low (0V) the output resistance (R4) will be high (not conducting).

5. When the potential divider circuit has one average (a few KOhm) input resistance (R3) and one high (not conducting) input resistance (R4) then the output voltage (V7) is high (9V).

6. Anyway, we were in the middle of explaining how the low heat warning circuit works if it has the following inputs: heat intensity high.

7. When the input voltage (V7) of the lamp is high (9V) the output brightness (B1) will be high (lamp on).

8. So, When the input heat intensity (H1) of the low heat warning circuit is low (cold) the output brightness (B1) will be high (lamp on).

9. When it is high (hot) the output brightness (B1) will be low (lamp off).

10. Is that enough about how the low heat warning circuit works?

U: 11. What does the comparator do?

S: 12. OK, When the input voltage (V2) of the comparator is quite high (towards 9V) the output voltage (V5) will be low (0V).

13. When it is quite low (towards 0V) the output voltage (V5) will be high (9V).

Anyway, is that enough about that?

U: 14. How does the comparator work?

S: 15. OK, suppose the input voltage is quite high (towards 9V).
[...]

16. Anyway, is that enought about that?

U: 17. OK.

This dialogue shows how errors may be explained and problems dealt with in follow-up questions. There are no major problems with the interaction, yet the explanation is still weak compared with human explanations. This seems largely due to the simplicity of the underlying models explaining everything in terms of inputs and outputs.

C.3   User D: Managing Interruptions

This example shows two remediation strategies being used, and the problems when the user asks consecutive questions! The first remediation strategy is clear and apparently helpful (lines 4–12). The second is based on over-simple models and is not so good (lines 16–18). In line 19 the user interprets the question "what's a comparator" differently from the system, so needs to ask another question (what it does). This

again is not really answered adequately due to the over-simple models
— a more appropriate answer might be "A comparator is a device which
compares its two inputs and gives either a high or low voltage depending
on which is greater." In the middle of the system's response the user
(accidentally?) asks the question again. The system correctly recognizes
this and avoids the repeated question. However, the two successive user
questions ("What's a comparator?" and "What does a comparator do?")
are treated as nested interruptions and result in an incorrect resumption
of two "anyway"s (lines 27–28).

S: 1. Suppose the input heat intensity is high (hot)?
   2. What's the output voltage (V2) of the heat detector circuit going to be
      when the input heat intensity is high (hot).
U: 3. Low (0V).
S: 4. Wrong, not quite, OK,
      A heat detector circuit is much like a light detector circuit only:
   5. – Its output voltage depends on the input light intensity.
   6. – It has a thermistor instead of a light-dependent resistor.
   7. This component here is a thermistor.
   8. Let's go through what a thermistor does.
      When the input heat intensity (H1) of the thermistor is high (hot) the
      output resistance (R1) will be quite low.
   9. When it is low (cold) the output resistance (R1) will be quite high.
  10. So, what's the output voltage (V2) of the heat detector circuit going to
      be when the input heat intensity is high (hot)?
U: 11. Quite high (towards 9V).
S: 12. Precisely, very good, it's quite high (towards 9V).
U: 13. Anyway, we were in the middle of explaining how the low heat warning
      device works if it has the following inputs: heat intensity high.
  14. What's the output voltage (V5) of the comparator going to be when
      the input voltage (V2) is quite high (towards 9V)?
U: 15. Quite high.
S: 16. Wrong, you lose,
      OK, maybe we better go through what a comparator does when it has
      a highish input voltage.
      Suppose the input voltage is quite high.
  17. When the operational amplifier has one medium (about 4.5V) input
      voltage (V3) and one quite high input voltage (V2) then the output
      voltage (V5) is low (0V).
  18. Anyway, we were in the middle of explaining how the low heat warning
      device works if it has the following inputs: heat intensity.

U: 19. What's a comparator?

S: 20. OK, this circuit section here is a comparator.

U: 21. What does a comparator do?

S: 22. OK, when the input voltage (V2) of the comparator is quite high (towards 9V) the output voltage (V5) will be low (0V).

U: 23. What does a comparator do?

S: 24. I'm in the middle of saying that. Do you want it answered right now?

U: 25. No.

S: 26. When it is quite low (towards 0V) the output voltage (V5) will be high (9V).

    27. Anyway, we were in the middle of explaining how the low heat warning device works if it has the following inputs: heat intensity high.

    28. Anyway, we were in the middle of explaining how the low heat warning device works if it has the following inputs: heat intensity high.

    29. What's the output voltage ʼof the inverter [...]

C.4   User J: Repeated Explanations

This example illustrates what happens when the user asks for a circuit to be explained for a second time. The first time the circuit was explained, relatively few questions were asked by the system but several by the user. The system has therefore built up a set of assumptions about what the user may know, and in the dialogue below it checks these assumptions by questioning the user.

The example also includes a sequence where the user asks a question following a system question, illustrating how the discourse is resumed by repeating the question.

S: 1. OK, we're going to be explaining how the light detector circuit works. It is a sort of potential divider circuit.

   2. Let's go through what the potential divider circuit does.
   What's the output voltage (in the middle of) the potential divider circuit going to be when there is a low (fully conducting) input resistance (near 9V rail) and a high (not conducting) input resistance (near 0V rail)?

U: 3. Quite high (towards 9V).

S: 4. No, I'm afraid not, it's high (9V).
   When it has one high (not conducting) input resistance (near 9V rail) and one low (fully conducting) input resistance (near 0V rail) then it is low (0V).

5. Can you tell me what the output voltage of the light detector circuit depends on?

U: 6. Light intensity.

S: 7. Yes, splendid, it's light intensity.
This component here is a light-dependent resistor.

8. Let's go through what the light-dependent resistor does.
When the input light intensity (L1) of the light-dependent resistor is high (light) the output resistance (R1) will be quite low.

9. What's it going to be when the input light intensity (L1) is low (dark)?

U: 10. Quite high.

S: 11. Yes, splendid, it's quite high.
OK, we're going to explain the behavior of the light detector circuit.
Suppose the input light intensity is high (light).

12. When the input light intensity (L1) of the light-dependent resistor is high (light) the output resistance (R1) will be quite low.

13. What's the output voltage (V1) of the potential divider circuit going to be when there is a quite high input resistance (R1) and a average (a few KOhm) input resistance (R2)?

U: 14. Quite high.

S: 15. Correct, great, it's quite high.
Suppose the input light intensity is low (dark).

16. When the input light intensity (L1) of the light-dependent resistor is low (dark) the output resistance (R1) will be quite high.

17. What's the output voltage (V1) of the potential divider circuit going to be when there is a quite low input resistance (R1) and a average (a few KOhm) input resistance (R2)?

U: 18. Quite low.

S: 19. Precisely, very good, it's quite low.
So, What's it going to be when the input light intensity (L1) is high (light)?

U: 20. Quite low (towards 0V).

S: 21. No, you lose, it's quite high (towards 0V).
What's it going to be when the input light intensity (L1) is low (dark)?

U: 22. What's a resistor?

S: 23. OK, this component here is a resistor.

24. Anyway, what's the output voltage (V1) of the light detector circuit going to be when the input light intensity (L1) is low (dark)?

U: 25. Quite low (towards 0V).

S: 26. Precisely, excellent, it's quite low.
Is that enough about how the light detector circuit works?

U: 27. OK.

At the end of the session the system had concluded that the user knows what a potential divider circuit and a light-dependent resistor do. It also adjusted its assessment of the user's level of expertise. For example, when the user asked "what's a resistor?" this caused the level to be decreased because the user is asking an easy question.

D Example Displays

The figures below are example screen displays when the low heat warning
device is explained. The first shows the system asking the user a question
as part of its causal explanation of the circuit.

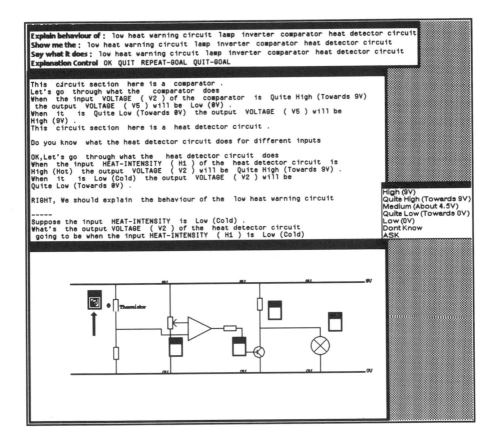

The second example shows how the user can ask questions from the
diagram. A question menu is displayed if the user points at a particular
component — in this case a transistor.

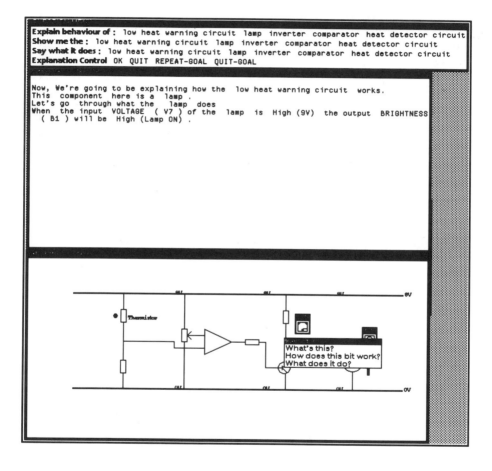

Bibliography

[AC87]   P. Agre and D. Chapman. Pengi: An implementation of a theory of
           activity. In *Proceedings of the Sixth National Conference on Artificial
           Intelligence*, Philadelphia, Pa., 1987.

[AP80]   J.F. Allen and C.R. Perrault. Analyzing intention in utterances. *Ar-
           tificial Intelligence*, 15:143–178, 1980.

[App85]   D.E. Appelt. *Planning English Sentences*. Cambridge University
           Press, Cambridge, UK, 1985.

[Aus75]   J.L. Austin. *How to Do Things with Words*. Clarendon Press, Oxford,
           UK, 1975.

[Bak89]   M. Baker. A model for tutorial dialogues based on critical argument. In
           D. Bierman, J. Breuker, and J. Sandberg, editors, *Artificial Intelligence
           and Education*, pages 2–8, Amsterdam, Netherlands, 1989. IOS.

[Bil91]   E. Bilange. A task independent oral dialogue model. In *Proceedings of
           the Fifth Conference of the European Chapter of the Association for
           Computational Linguistics*, pages 83–88, Berlin, Germany, 1991.

[Bla90]   A. Blandford. A model for the generation of tutorial dialogue. Techni-
           cal Report 121, Centre for Information Technology in Education, Open
           University, 1990.

[Bur81]   D. Burton. Analysing spoken discourse. In M. Coulthard and
           M. Montgomery, editors, *Studies in Discourse Analysis*, pages 61–81.
           Routledge and Kegan Paul, London, 1981.

[BW79]   J.B. Black and R. Wilensky. An evaluation of story grammars. *Cog-
           nitive Science*, 3:213–230, 1979.

[BWS87]   J. Breuker, R. Winkels, and J. Sandberg. A shell for intelligent help
           systems. In *Proceedings of the Tenth International Conference on Ar-
           tificial Intelligence*, pages 167–173, Milan, Italy, 1987.

[Car70]   J.R. Carbonell. AI in CAI: An artificial intelligence approach to com-
           puter assisted instruction. *IEEE Transactions on Man Machine Sys-
           tems*, 11(4):190–202, 1970.

[Car83]   L. Carlson. *Dialogue Games: An Approach to Discourse Analysis*. D.
           Reidel Pub. Co., Dordrecht, Holland; Boston, 1983.

[Car89]   S. Carberry. Plan recognition and its use in understanding dialog. In
           A. Kobsa and W. Wahlster, editors, *User Models in Dialog Systems*,
           pages 133–162. Springer Verlag, Berlin, 1989.

[Car92]   J.C. Carletta. *Risk-taking and Recovery in Task-oriented Dialogues*.
           PhD thesis, Department of Artificial Intelligence, University of Edin-
           burgh, 1992.

[Caw91]   A. Cawsey. Generating interactive explanations. In *Proceedings of
           the Ninth National Conference on Artificial Intelligence*, pages 86–91,
           Anaheim, Calif., 1991.

[Caw92]   A. Cawsey. Planning interactive explanations. *International Journal
           of Man-Machine Studies*, 1992.

[CC77]   H.H. Clark and E.V. Clark. *Psychology and Language: An Introduc-
           tion to Psycholinguistics*. Harcourt Brace Jovanovich, New York, 1977.

[Chi89]   D. Chin. Knome: Modeling what the user knows in uc. In A. Kobsa
           and W. Wahlster, editors, *User Models in Dialog Systems*, pages 74–
           107. Springer Verlag, Berlin, 1989.

[CJP88]   B. Cox, J. Jenkins, and E. Pollitzer. An explanation-driven, understanding-directed user model for intelligent tutoring systems. *IEE Colloquium on Intelligent Tutoring Systems*, pages 4/1–4/3, 1988.

[CL91]   P.R. Cohen and H.J. Levesque. Teamwork. *Nous*, 25, 1991.

[CMN83]   S.K. Card, T.P. Moran, and A. Newell. *The Psychology of Human Computer Interaction*. Lawrence Erlbaum, Hillsdale, N.J.; London, 1983.

[CMP90]   P.R. Cohen, J. Morgan, and M.E. Pollack. *Intentions in Communication*. The MIT Press, Cambridge, Mass., 1990.

[CS82]   A. Collins and A.L. Stevens. Goal strategies of inquiry teachers. In R.Glaser, editor, *Advances in Instructional Psychology*, volume 2. Lawrence Erlbaum, Hillsdale, 1982.

[CS89]   H.H. Clark and E.F. Schaefer. Contributing to discourse. *Cognitive Science*, 13:259–294, 1989.

[Dal88]   R. Dale. *Generating Referring Expressions in a Domain of Objects and Processes*. PhD thesis, Center for Cognitive Science, University of Edinburgh, 1988.

[dBD81]   R. de Beaugrande and W.U. Dressler. *Introduction to Text Linguistics*. Longman, London, 1981.

[dK84]   J. de Kleer. How circuits work. *Artificial Intelligence*, 24:205–280, 1984.

[dK86]   J. de Kleer. An assumption based truth maintenance system. *Artificial Intelligence*, 28:127–190, 1986.

[Dra88]   S.W. Draper. What's going on in everyday explanation? In *Analysing Everyday Explanation*, pages 15–31. SAGE, London, 1988.

[FF88]   B. Falkenheiner and K.D. Forbus. Setting up large-scale qualitative models. In *Proceedings of the Sixth National Conference on Artificial Intelligence*, pages 301–306, St. Paul, Minn., 1988.

[FI85]   P.E. Friedland and Y. Iwasaki. The concept and implementation of skeletal plans. *Journal of Automated Reasoning*, 1:161–208, 1985.

[Fin89]   T. Finin. Gums — a general user modeling shell. In A. Kobsa and W. Wahlster, editors, *User Models in Dialog Systems*, pages 411–440. Springer Verlag, Berlin, 1989.

[FL90]   D. Frohlich and P. Luff. Applying the technology of conversation to the technology for conversation. In P. Luff, D. Frohlich, and N. Gilbert, editors, *Computers and Conversation*, pages 187–220. Academic Press, London, 1990.

[FM90]   S. Feiner and K.R. McKeown. Coordinating text and graphics in explanation generation. In *Proceedings of the Eighth National Conference on Artificial Intelligence*, pages 442–449, Boston, Mass., 1990.

[Fox87]   B.A. Fox. Interactional reconstruction in real-time language processing. *Cognitive Science*, 11:365–388, 1987.

[FR86]   G. Ferrari and R. Reilly. A two level dialogue representation. *Proceedings of the Eleventh International Conference on Computational Linguistics*, pages 42–45, 1986.

[FS81]   K.D. Forbus and A.L. Stevens. Using qualitative simulations to gener-
              ate explanations. Technical Report 4490, Bolt Beranek and Newman,
              Inc., Cambridge, Mass., 1981.

[Geo90]   M.P. Georgeff. Planning. In J. Allen, J. Hendler, and A. Tate, editors,
              Readings in Planning. Morgan Kaufmann Publishers, Inc., Los Altos,
              California, 1990.

[Gil87]   G.N. Gilbert. Advice, discourse and explanations. In *Proceedings of
              the Third Alvey Explanation Workshop*, 1987. (Available from the
              DTI, London).

[GJ92]   J.R. Galliers and K. Sparck Jones. Evaluating natural language pro-
              cessing systems. Technical report, Computer Laboratory, University
              of Cambridge, 1992.

[Gri75]   H.P. Grice. Logic and conversation. In P. Cole and J. Morgan, editors,
              Syntax and Semantics III: Speech Acts, pages 41–58. Academic Press,
              New York, 1975.

[Gro77]   B. Grosz. The representation and use of focus in dialog understanding.
              Technical Report 151, Artificial Intelligence Center, SRI International,
              Menlo Park, Calif., 1977.

[GS86]   B.J. Grosz and C.L. Sidner. Attention, intentions, and the structure
              of discourse. *Computational Linguistics*, 12(3):175–204, 1986.

[GS90]   B.J. Grosz and C.L. Sidner. Plans for discourse. In P.R. Cohen, J. Mor-
              gan, and M.E. Pollack, editors, *Intentions in Communication*, pages
              417–444. The MIT Press, Cambridge, Mass., 1990.

[HA91]   E.H. Hovy and Y. Arens. Automatic generation of formatted text.
              In *Proceedings of the Ninth National Conference on Artificial Intelli-
              gence*, pages 92–97, Anaheim, Calif., 1991.

[Har88]   S. Harris. Court discourse as genre: some problems and issues. In R.P.
              Fawcett, editor, *New Developments in Systemic Linguistics: Theory
              and Application*, pages 94–115. Francis Pinter, London, 1988.

[HE79]   J.R. Hobbs and D. Evans. Conversation as planned behavior. Techni-
              cal Report 203, Artificial Intelligence Center, SRI International, Menlo
              Park, Calif., 1979.

[HH76]   M.A.K. Halliday and R. Hasan. *Cohesion in English*. Longman, Lon-
              don, 1976.

[HH89]   M.A.K. Halliday and R. Hasan. *Language, Context and Text: Aspects
              of Language in a Social-semiotic Perspective*. Oxford University Press,
              Oxford, UK, 1989.

[HI85]   G. Houghton and S. Isard. Why to speak, what to say and how to
              say it : Modelling language production in discourse. In *Proceedings
              of the International Workshop on Modelling Cognition*, University of
              Lancaster, 1985.

[HMGN91]   X. Huang, G.I. McCalla, J.E. Greer, and E. Neufeld. Revising deduc-
              tive knowledge and stereotype knowledge in a student model. *User
              Modeling and User-Adapted Interaction*, 1(1):87–116, 1991.

[Hob83]   J.R. Hobbs. Towards an understanding of coherence in discourse. In
              M. Brady and R.C. Berwick, editors, *Computational Models of Dis-
              course*, pages 223–243. The MIT Press, Cambridge, Mass., 1983.

[Hov88]   E.H. Hovy. Planning coherent multisentential text. In *Proceedings of the Twenty-sixth Anual Meeting of the Association for Computational Linguistics*, pages 163–169, Buffalo, New York, 1988.

[Hov90]   E.H. Hovy. Pragmatics and natural language generation. *Artificial Intelligence*, 43(2):153–197, 1990.

[Jef72]   G. Jefferson. Side sequences. In D. Sudnow, editor, *Studies in Social Interaction*, pages 294–338. Macmillan, New York, 1972.

[JM89]   C. Jullien and J.C. Marty. Plan revision in person-machine dialogue. In *Proceedings of the Fourth Conference of the European Chapter of the Association for Computational Linguistics*, pages 153–160, Manchester, England, 1989.

[Joh87]   A. Johnson. *Electronics: A Systems Approach*. Hodder and Stoughton, London, 1987.

[Jon91]   K. Sparck Jones. Discourse modelling: where we are now, and where should we be going? In *Working Notes: AAAI Fall Symposium on Discourse Structure in Natural Language Understanding and Generation*, pages 142–145, Monterey, Calif., 1991.

[Ken83]   A. Kendon. Gesture and speech : How they interact. In J.M. Wiemann and R.P. Harrison, editors, *Nonverbal Interaction*. Sage, Beverly Hills; London, 1983.

[KF87]   R. Kass and T. Finin. Rules for the implicit acquisition of knowledge about the user. In *Proceedings of the Sixth National Conference on Artificial Intelligence*, pages 295–300, Seattle, WA, 1987.

[KF88]   R. Kass and T. Finin. Modeling the user in natural language systems. *Computational Linguistics*, 14(3):5–22, 1988.

[Kie85]   D.E. Kieras. Thematic processes in the comprehension of technical prose. In B.J. Britton and J.B. Black, editors, *Understanding Expository Text : A Theoretical and Practical Handbook for Analyzing Explanatory Text*. Lawrence Erlbaum, 1985.

[KKR91]   R. Kittredge, T. Korelsky, and O. Rambow. On the need of domain communication knowledge. *Computational Intelligence*, 7:305–314, 1991.

[KW89]   A. Kobsa and W. Wahlster, editors. *User Models in Dialog Systems*. Springer Verlag, Berlin, 1989.

[LA87]   D.L. Litman and J.F. Allen. A plan recognition model for subdialogs in conversations. *Cognitive Science*, 11:163–200, 1987.

[Les88]   A. Lesgold. Towards a theory of curriculum design for use in Intelligent Instructional Systems. In H. Mandl and A. Lesgold, editors, *Learning Issues for Intelligent Tutoring Systems*, pages 114–137. Springer Verlag, New York, 1988.

[Lev83]   S. C. Levinson. *Pragmatics*. Cambridge University Press, Cambridge, UK, 1983.

[Man87]   W.C. Mann. Text generation: The problem of text structure. Technical Report ISI/RS-87-181, University of Southern California, 1987.

[May91a]   M.T. Maybury. Planning multi-media explanations using communicative acts. In *Proceedings of the Ninth National Conference on Artificial Intelligence*, pages 61–66, Anaheim, Calif., 1991.

[May91b]   M.T. Maybury. *Planning Multisentential English Text Using Communicative Acts.* PhD thesis, Computer Laboratory, University of Cambridge, 1991. Published as technical report 239, Computer Laboratory, University of Cambridge.

[MC91]   K.F. McCoy and J. Cheng. Focus of attention: Constraining what can be said next. In C.L. Paris, W.R. Swartout, and W.C. Mann, editors, *Natural Language Generation in Artificial Intelligence and Computational Linguistics*, pages 103–124. Kluwer Academic, Dordrecht, Netherlands, 1991.

[McC89]   Kathleen F. McCoy. Generating context-sensitive responses to object related misconceptions. *Artificial Intelligence*, 41(2), December 1989.

[McK85]   K.R. McKeown. *Text Generation: Using discourse strategies and focus constraints to generate natural language text.* Cambridge University Press, 1985.

[McK88]   K.R. McKeown. Generating goal-oriented explanations. *International Journal of Expert Systems Research and Applications*, 4:377–395, 1988.

[MCM91]   D.J. Mooney, S. Carberry, and K.F. McCoy. Capturing high level structure of naturally occuring, extended explanations using bottom-up strategies. *Computational Intelligence*, 7:334–356, 1991.

[Mee76]   J.R. Meehan. *The Metanovel: Writing Stories by Computer.* PhD thesis, Yale University, 1976.

[MF91]   I. Markova and K. Foppa, editors. *Asymmetries in Dialogue.* Harvester Wheatsheaf, Hemel Hemstead, UK, 1991.

[Miy86]   N. Miyake. Constructive interaction and the iterative process of understanding. *Cognitive Science*, 10:151–177, 1986.

[MJ80]   J.M. Mandler and N.S. Johnson. On throwing out the baby with the bathwater: A reply to Black and Wilensky's evaluation of story grammars. *Cognitive Science*, 4:305–312, 1980.

[MM81]   W.C. Mann and J.A. Moore. Computer generation of multiparagraph text. *American Journal of Computational Linguistics*, 7:17–29, 1981.

[Moo89]   J.D. Moore. *A Reactive Approach to Explanation in Expert and Advice-Giving Systems.* PhD thesis, University of California, Los Angeles, 1989. (published as Technical Report ISI-SR-90-251, USC/Information Sciences Institute).

[Moo91]   J.D. Moore. A reacting approach to explanation: Taking the user's feedback into account. In C.L. Paris, W.R. Swartout, and W.C. Mann, editors, *Natural Language Generation in Artificial Intelligence and Computational Linguistics*, pages 3–48. Kluwer Academic, Dordrecht, Netherlands, 1991.

[MP89]   J.D. Moore and C.L. Paris. Planning text for advisory dialogues. In *Proceedings of the Twenty-Seventh Annual Meeting of the Association for Computational Linguistics*, pages 67–75, Vancouver, Canada, 1989.

[MS90]   J.D. Moore and W.R. Swartout. Pointing: A way towards explanation dialogue. In *Proceedings of the Eighth National Conference on Artificial Intelligence*, pages 457–464, Anaheim, Calif., 1990.

[MT87a]   W.C. Mann and S.A. Thompson. Rhetorical structure theory: A framework for the analysis of texts. Technical Report RS-87-190, USC/Information Sciences Institute, 1987.

[MT87b]   W.C. Mann and S.A. Thomson. Rhetorical structure theory: Description and construction of text structures. In Gerard Kempen, editor, *Natural Language Generation*, pages 83–96. Martinus Nijhoff, Dordrecht, Netherlands, 1987.

[Mur89]   W.R. Murray. Control for intelligent tutoring systems: A blackboard-based dynamic instructional planner. In D. Bierman, J. Breuker, and J. Sandberg, editors, *Artificial Intelligence and Education*, pages 150–168, Amsterdam, Netherlands, 1989. IOS.

[Par87]   C.L. Paris. Combining discourse strategies to generate descriptions to users along a naive/expert spectrum. In *Proceedings of the Tenth International Joint Conference on Artificial Intelligence*, pages 626–632, Milan, Italy, 1987.

[Par88]   C. Paris. Tailoring object descriptions to a user's level of expertise. *Computational Linguistics (Special Issue on User Modeling)*, 14(3):64–78, 1988.

[Par89]   C.L. Paris. The use of explicit user models in a generation system for tailoring answers to the user's level of expertise. In A. Kobsa and W. Wahlster, editors, *User Models in Dialog Systems*, pages 200–232. Springer Verlag, Berlin, 1989.

[PB89]   A. Petrie-Brown. Intelligent tutoring dialogue: The structures of an interaction. In D. Bierman, J. Breuker, and J. Sandberg, editors, *Artificial Intelligence and Education*, pages 195–201, Amsterdam, Netherlands, 1989. IOS.

[PM86]   D.R. Peachey and G.I. McCalla. Using planning techniques in intelligent tutoring systems. *International Journal of Man-Machine Studies*, 24:77–98, 1986.

[Pol87]   L. Polanyi. The linguistic discourse model: Towards a formal theory of discourse structure. Technical Report 6409, Bolt Beranek and Newman, Inc., Cambridge, Mass., 1987.

[Pow79]   R. Power. The organisation of purposeful dialogues. *Linguistics*, 17:107–152, 1979.

[Rei81]   R. Reichman. *Getting Computers to Talk Like You and Me*. The MIT Press, Cambridge, Mass., 1981.

[Ric79]   E. Rich. User modeling via stereotypes. *Cognitive Science*, 3:329–354, 1979.

[RML92]   E. Reiter, C. Mellish, and J. Levine. Automatic generation of on-line documentation in the IDAS project. In *Proceedings of the Third Conference on Applied Natural Language Processing*, pages 64–71, Trento, Itlay, 1992.

[Rum75]   D.E. Rumelhart. Notes on a schema for stories. In D. Bobrow and A. Collins, editors, *Representation and Understanding*, pages 211–238. Academic Press, New York, 1975.

[SC75]   J. McH. Sinclair and R.M. Coulthard. *Towards an Analysis of Discourse: The English Used by Teachers and Pupils*. Oxford University Press, London, 1975.

[Sch88]   E.A. Schegloff. Pre-sequences and indirection: Applying speech act theory to ordinary conversation. *Journal of Pragmatics*, 12:55–62, 1988.

[Sib91]   P. Sibun. *The Local Organization and Incremental Generation of Text.* PhD thesis, University of Massachusetts, 1991.

[Sid83]   C.L. Sidner. Focusing in the comprehension of definite anaphora. In M. Brady and R.C. Berwick, editors, *Computational Models of Discourse*, pages 267–330. The MIT Press, Cambridge, Mass., 1983.

[Sim85]   R. Simmons. Self explanatory device descriptions. *SIGART Newsletter*, 93:24–25, 1985.

[SJS77]   E.A. Schegloff, G. Jefferson, and H. Sacks. The preference for self-correction in the organization of repair in conversation. *Language*, 53:361–382, 1977.

[Sle85]   D. Sleeman. UMFE: A user modelling front end subsystem. *International Journal of Man-Machine Studies*, 23:71–88, 1985.

[SP90]   G. Schafer and J. Pearl, editors. *Readings in Uncertain Reasoning.* Morgan Kaufmann, San Mateo, California, 1990.

[SS81]   A.L. Stevens and C. Steinberg. A typology of explanations and its application to intelligent computer aided instruction. Technical Report 4626, Bolt Beranek and Newman, Inc., Cambridge, Mass., 1981.

[SSJ78]   H. Sacks, E.A. Schegloff, and G. Jefferson. A simplest systematics for the organization of turn taking in for conversation. In J.N. Schenkein, editor, *Studies in Organization of Conversational Interaction (Vol 1)*, pages 7–55. Academic Press, New York, 1978.

[Stu76]   M.J. Stubbs. Keeping in touch: Some functions of teacher-talk. In M. Stubbs and S. Delamont, editors, *Explorations in Classroom Observation*. Wiley, London; New York; Chichester, 1976.

[Suc87]   L. Suchman. *Plans and Situated Actions.* Cambridge University Press, Cambridge, UK, 1987.

[Sut89]   D.D. Suthers. Perspectives in explanation. Technical Report 89-24, Department of Computer and Information Science, University of Massachusetts, 1989.

[Sut91]   D.D. Suthers. A task-appropriate hybrid architecture for explanation. *Computational Intelligence*, 7:315–332, 1991.

[SY88]   T. Simon and R.M. Young. Goms meets strips: The integration of planning with skilled procedure execution in human-computer interaction. In D.M. Jones and R. Winder, editors, *People and Computers IV*, pages 581–594. Cambridge University Press, Cambridge, UK, 1988.

[Tra91]   D.R. Traum. The discourse reasoner in trains-90. TRAINS technical note 91-5, Department of Computer Science, University of Rochester, 1991.

[vD85]   T.A. van Dijk. Structures of news in the press. In T.A. van Dijk, editor, *Discourse and Communication: New Approaches to the Analysis of Mass Media Discourse and Communication*. W. de Gruyter, Berlin; New York, 1985.

[Wac86]   T. Wachtel. Pragmatic sensitivity in natural language interfaces and the structure of conversation. In *Proceedings of the Eleventh International Conference on Computational Linguistics*, pages 35–41, Bonn, Germany, 1986.

[WAGR91]   W. Wahlster, E. Andre, W. Graf, and T. Rist. Designing illustrated
            texts: How language production is influenced by graphics generation.
            In *Proceedings of the Fifth Conference of the European Chapter of the
            Association for Computational Linguistics*, pages 8–14, Berlin, Ger-
            many, 1991.

[Wal92]   M.A. Walker. Redundancy in collaborative dialogue. In *Proceedings
            of the Fourteenth International Conference on Computational Linguis-
            tics*, Nantes, France, 1992.

[WCL⁺88]   R. Wilensky, D.N. Chin, M. Luria, J. Martin, J. Mayfield, and D. Wu.
            The Berkeley UNIX consultant project. *Computational Linguistics*,
            14(4):35–84, 1988.

[Wei80]   J.L. Weiner. Blah, a system which explains its reasoning. *Artificial
            Intelligence*, 15:19–48, 1980.

[Wen87]   E. Wenger. *Artificial Intelligence and Tutoring Systems: Computa-
            tional Approaches to the Communication of Knowledge*. Morgan Kauf-
            mann, Los Altos, Calif., 1987.

[WF86]   B.Y. White and J.R. Frederiksen. Intelligent tutoring systems based
            upon qualitative model evolutions. *Proceedings of the Fifth National
            Conference on Artificial Intelligence*, pages 313–319, 1986.

[WK89]   W. Wahlster and A. Kobsa. User models in dialog systems. In *User
            Models in Dialog Systems*, pages 4–34. Springer Verlag, Berlin, 1989.

[WM87]   B. Woolf and T. Murray. A framework for representing tutorial dis-
            course. In *Proceedings of the Tenth International Conference on Ar-
            tificial Intelligence*, pages 189–192, Milan, Italy, 1987.

[Woo90]   R. Wooffitt. On the analysis of interaction: An introduction to con-
            versation analysis. In P. Luff, D. Frohlich, and N. Gilbert, editors,
            Computers and Conversation, pages 7–38. Academic Press, London,
            1990.

[WS85]   J.W. Wallis and E.H. Shortliffe. Customized explanations using causal
            knowledge. In B.G. Buchanan and E.H. Shortliffe, editors, *Rule Based
            Expert Systems: The MYCIN experiments of the Stanford Heuristic
            Programming Project*, pages 371–390. Addison Wesley, Reading, Mass.;
            London, 1985.

[ZP86]   I. Zukerman and J. Pearl. Comprehension-driven generation of meta-
            technical utterances in math tutoring. In *Proceedings of the the
            Fifth National Conference on Artificial Intelligence*, pages 606–611,
            Philadelphia, Pa., 1986.

Index